Mandala Magic
Coloring Book for Adults

By Nathalie Delmont

Copyright @ 2020 Carpe Diem Publishing

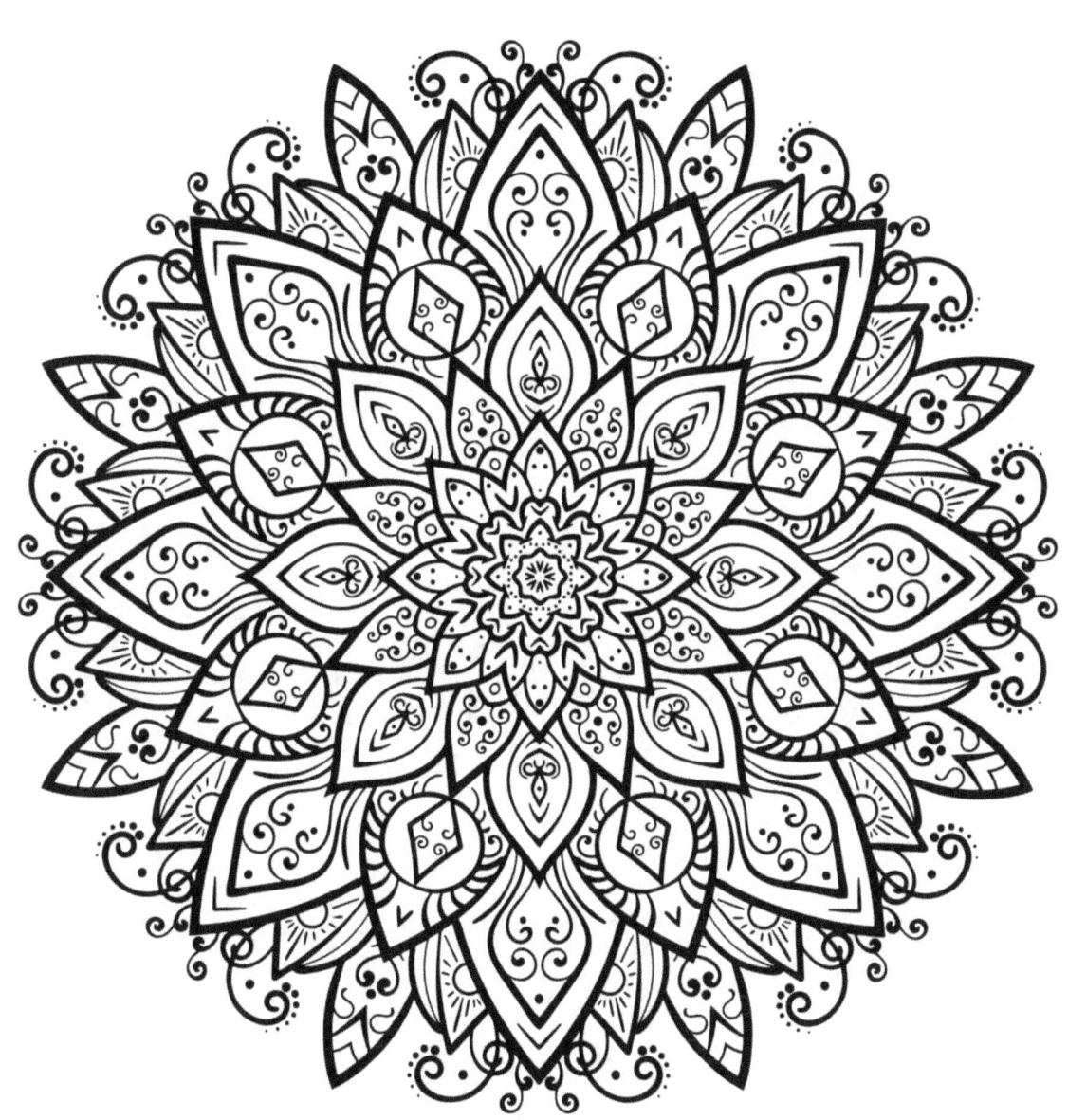

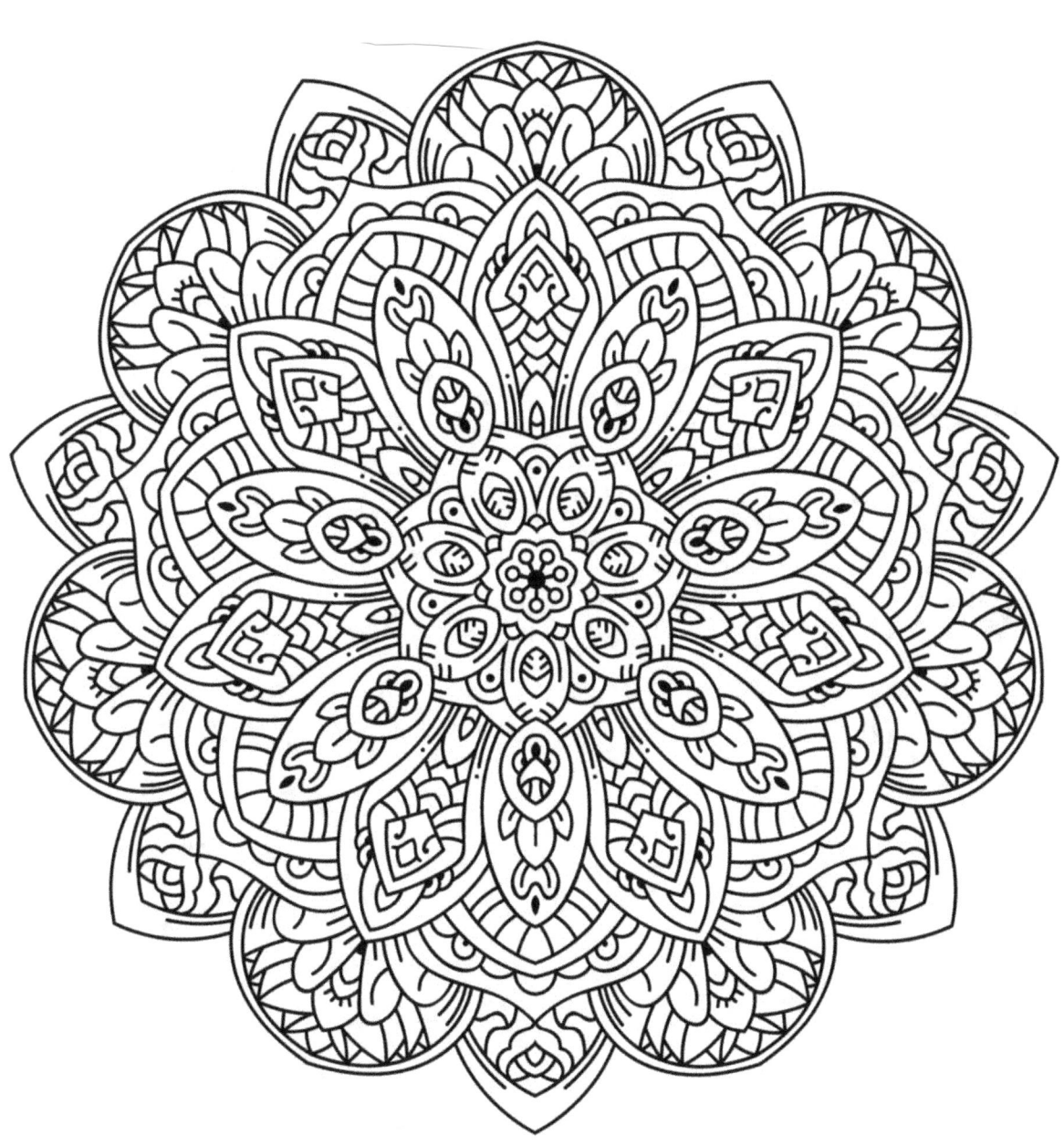

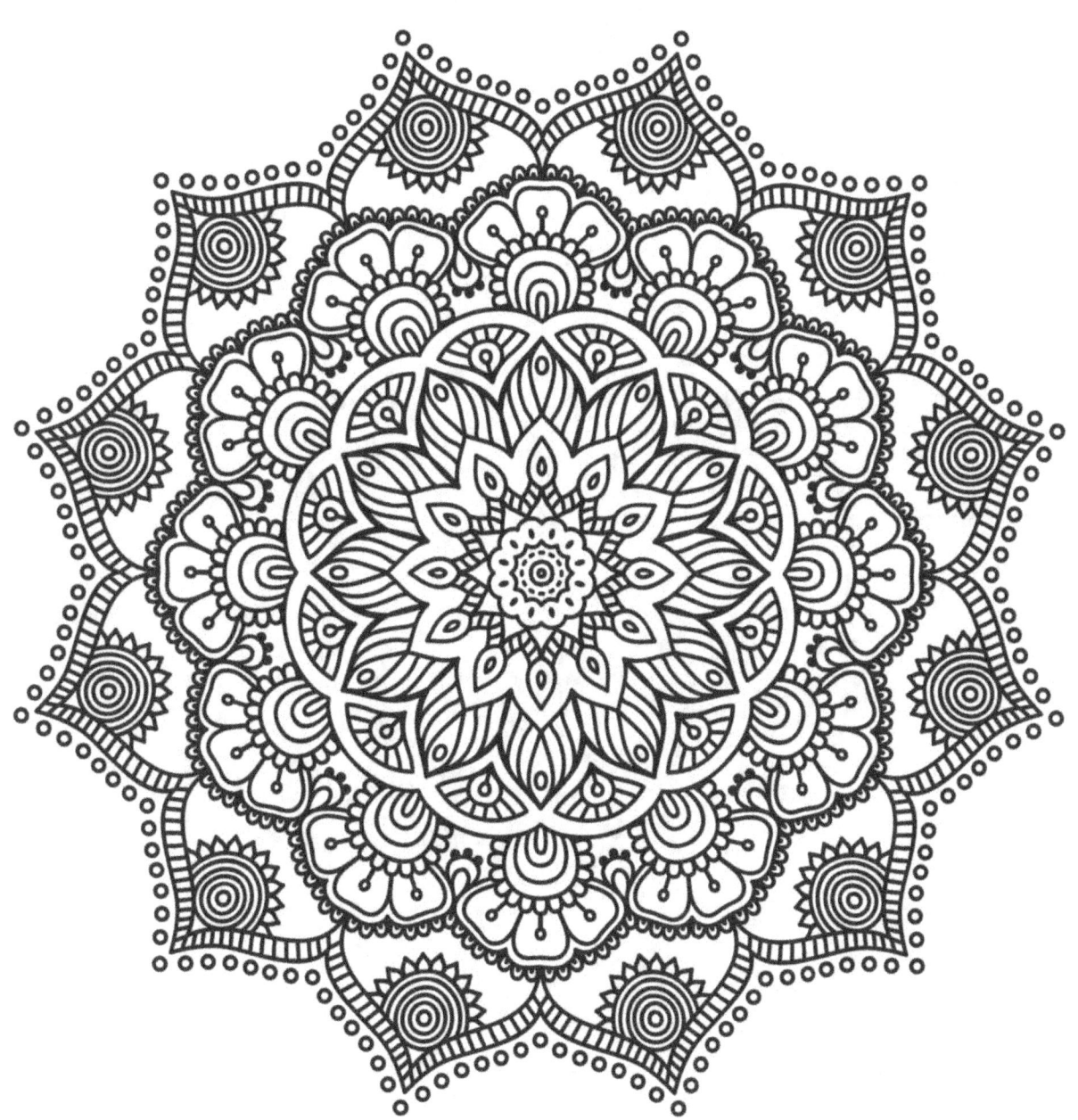

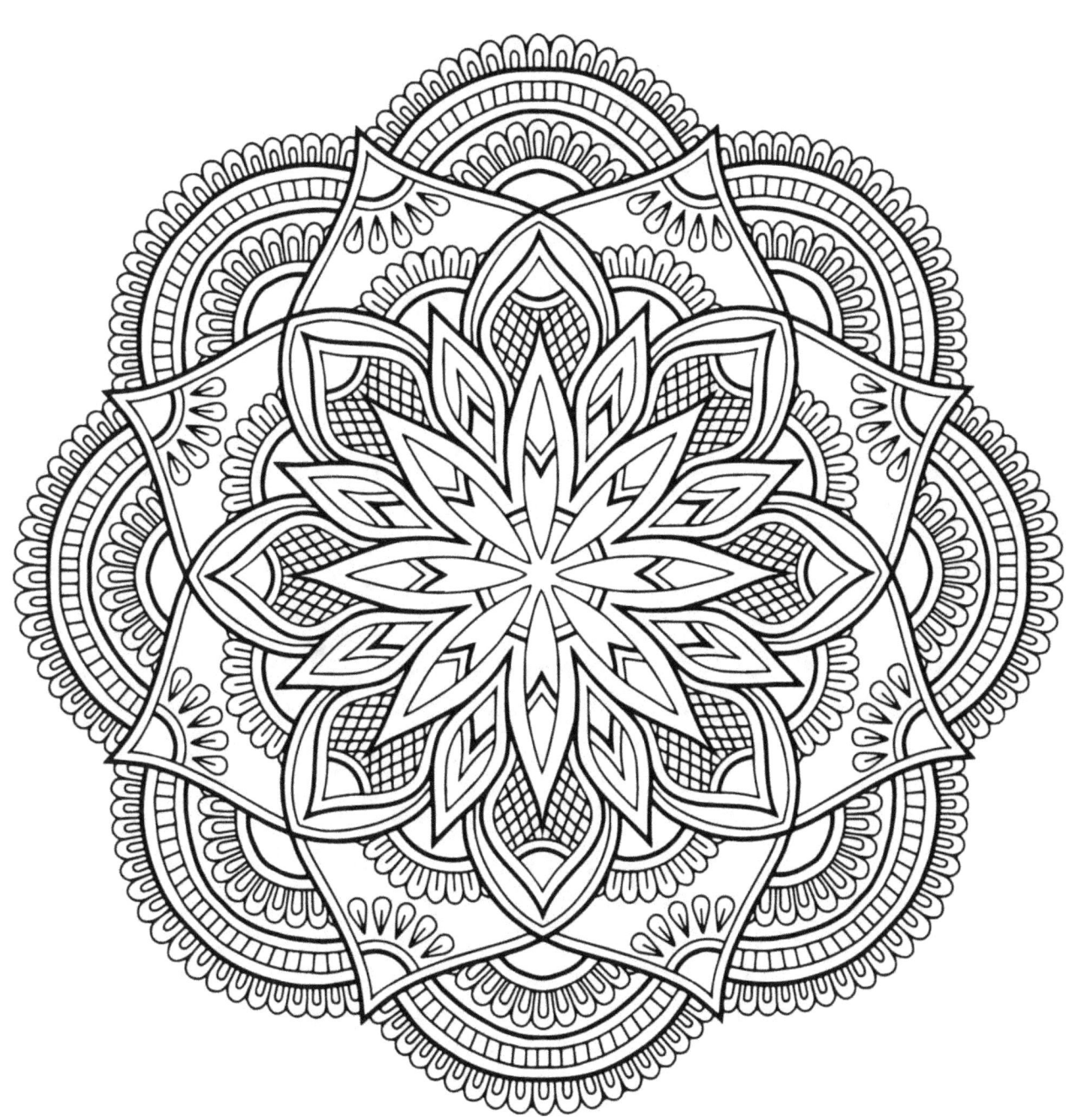

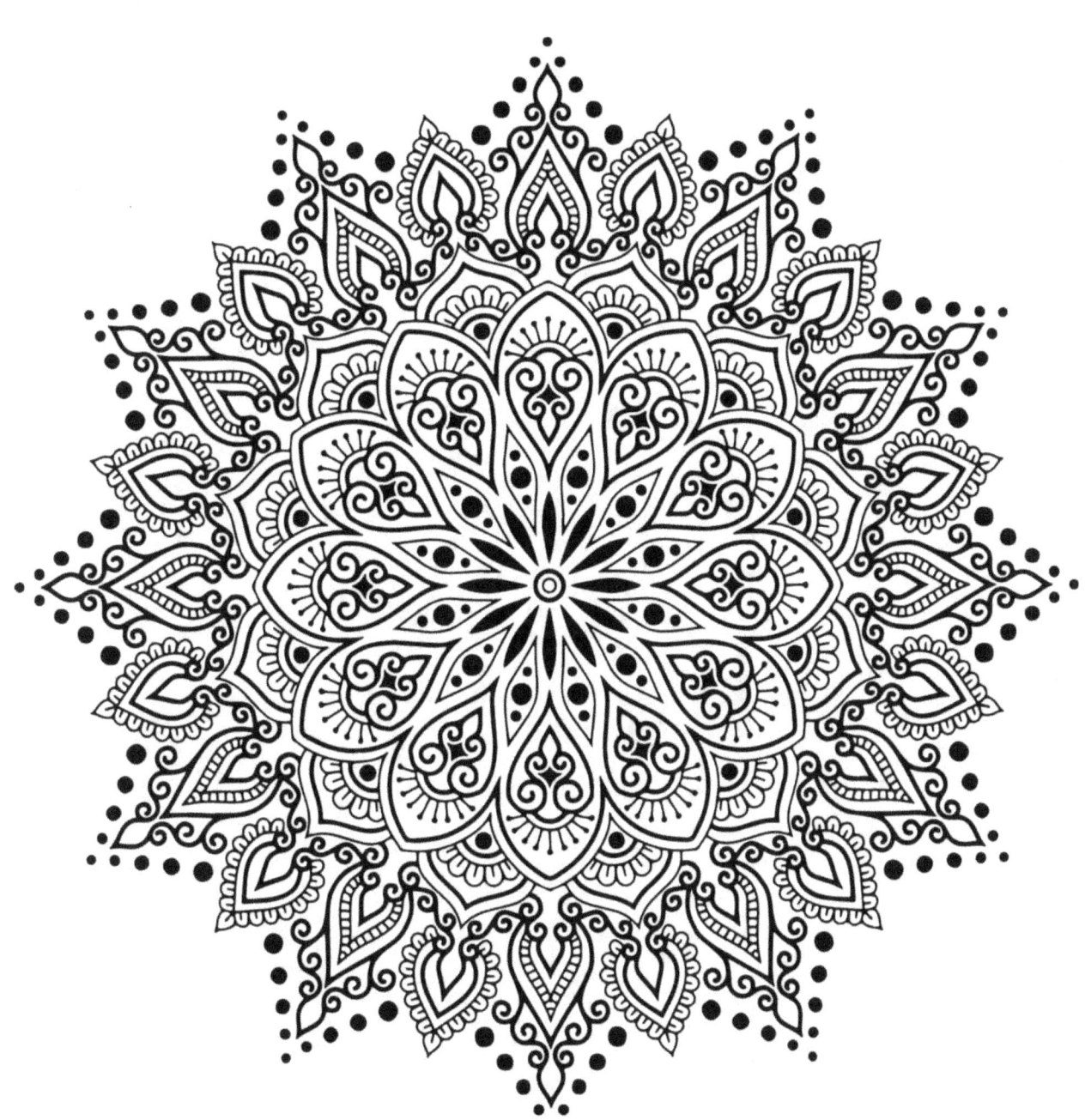

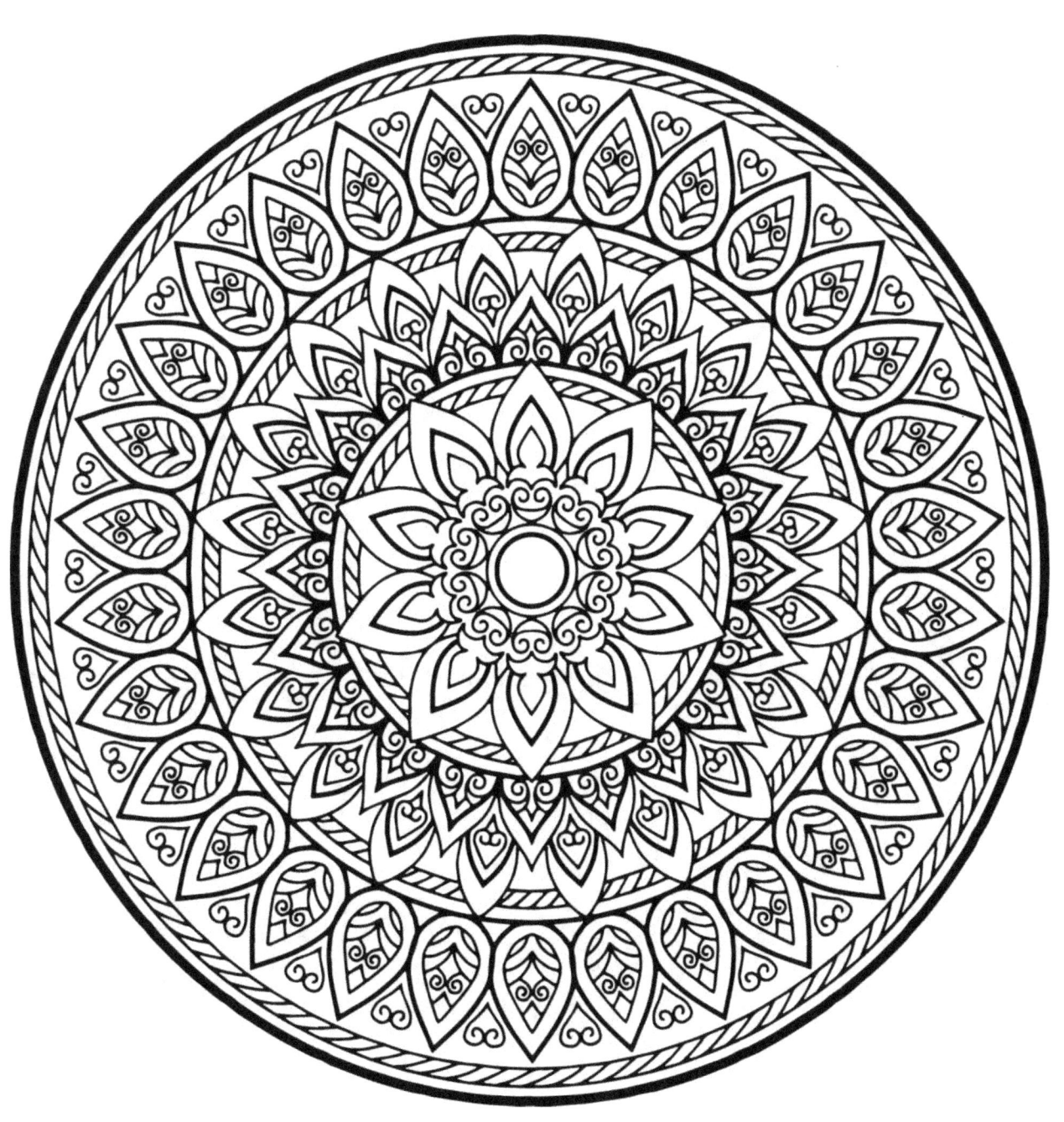

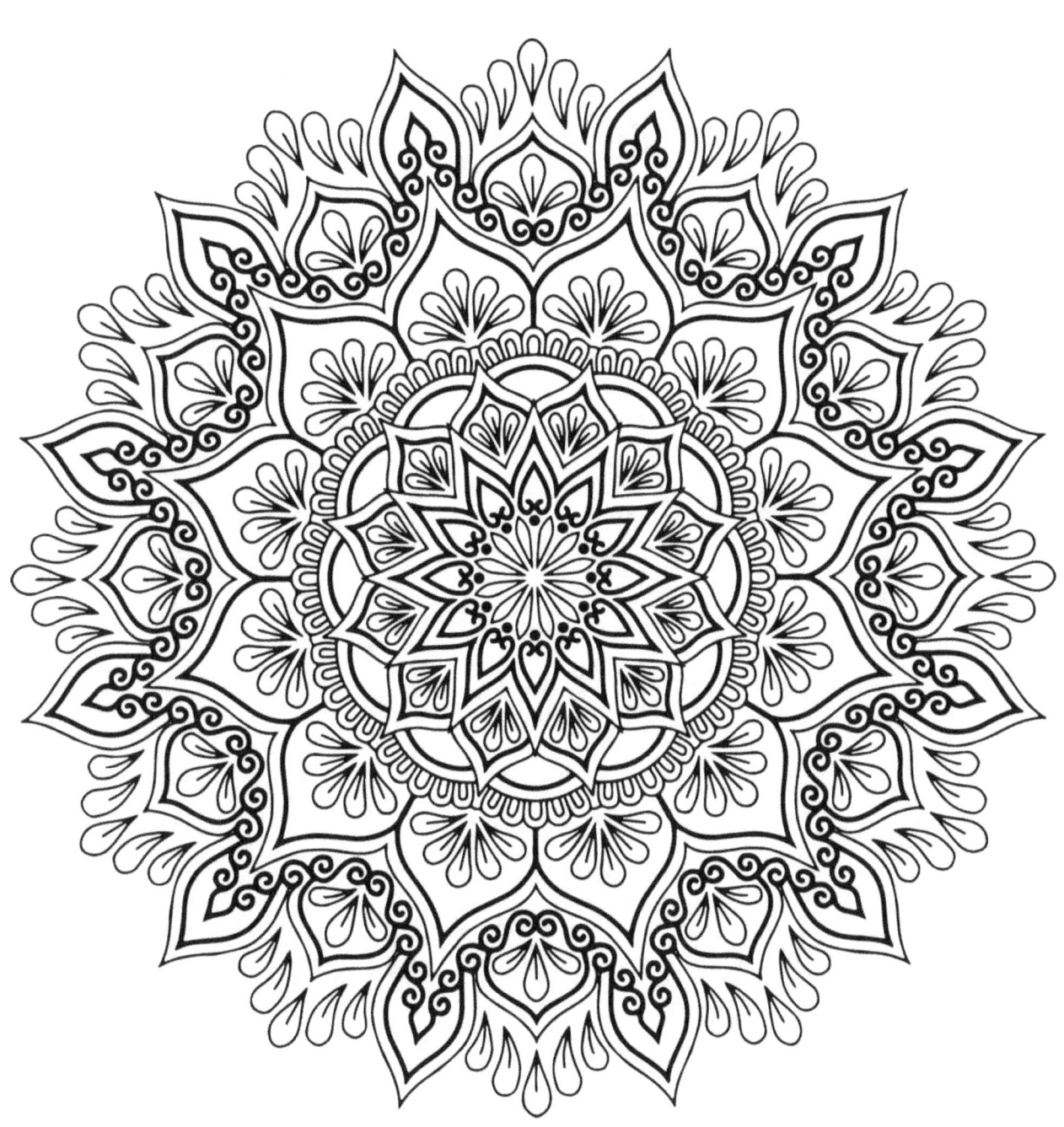

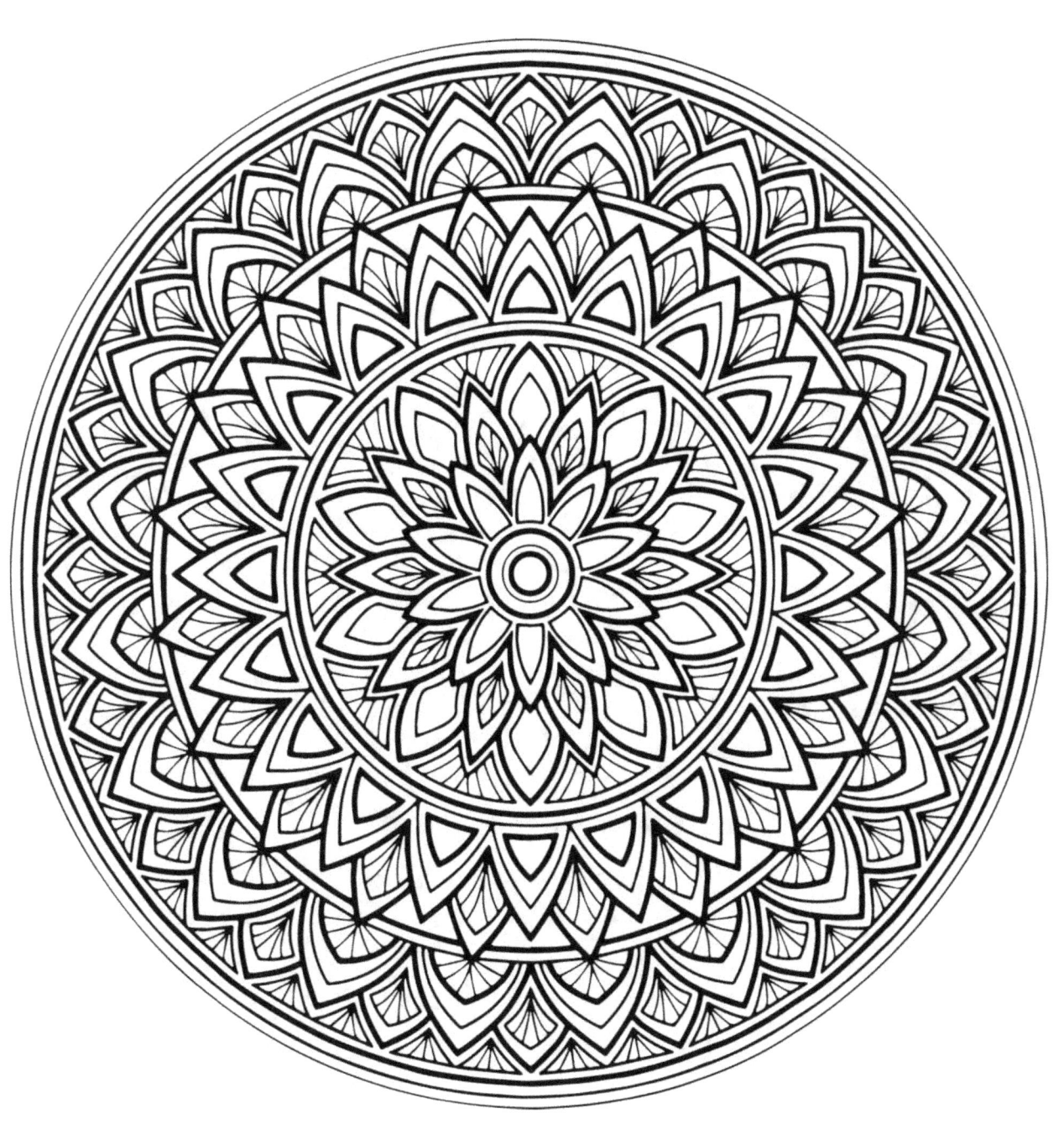

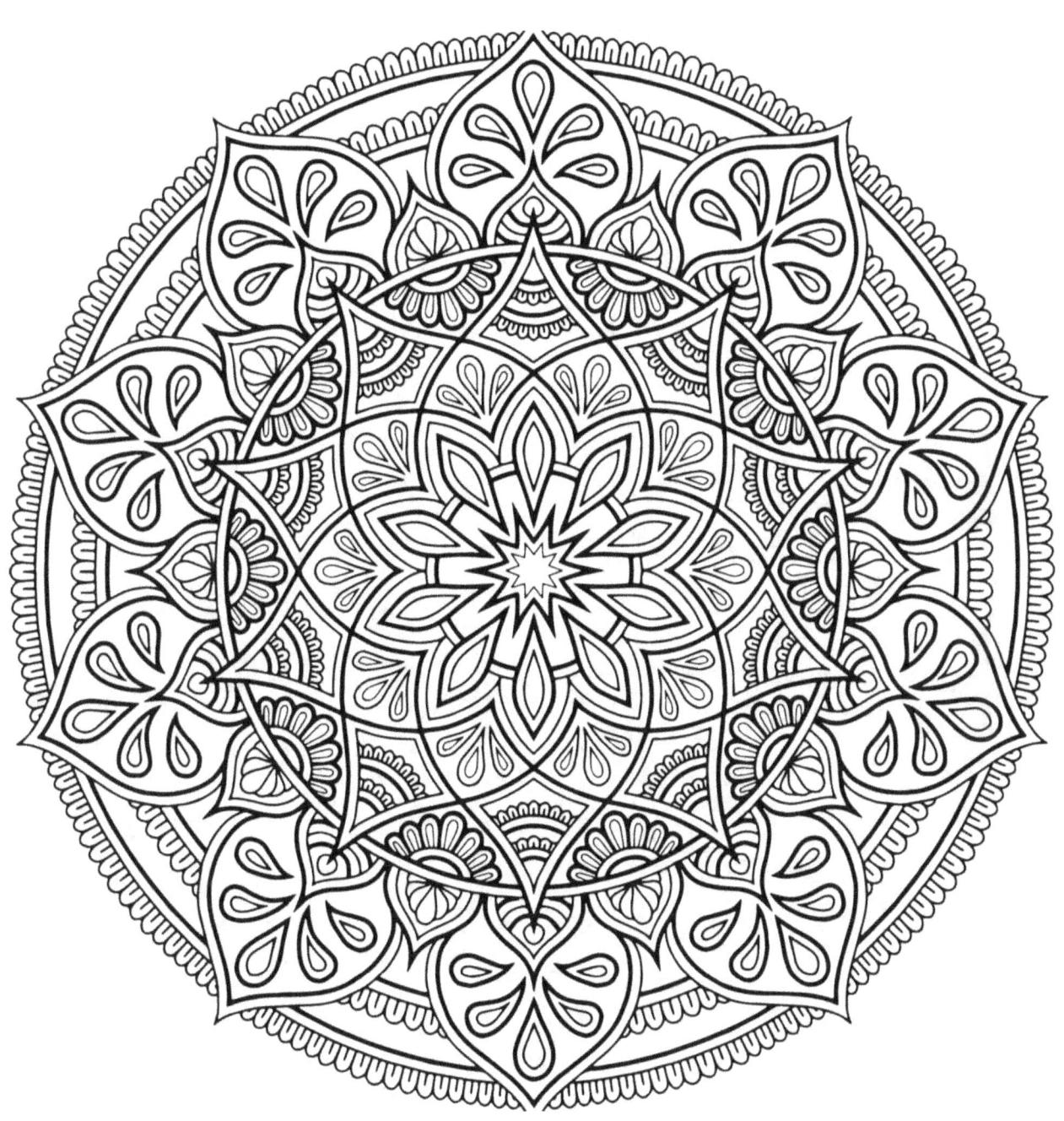

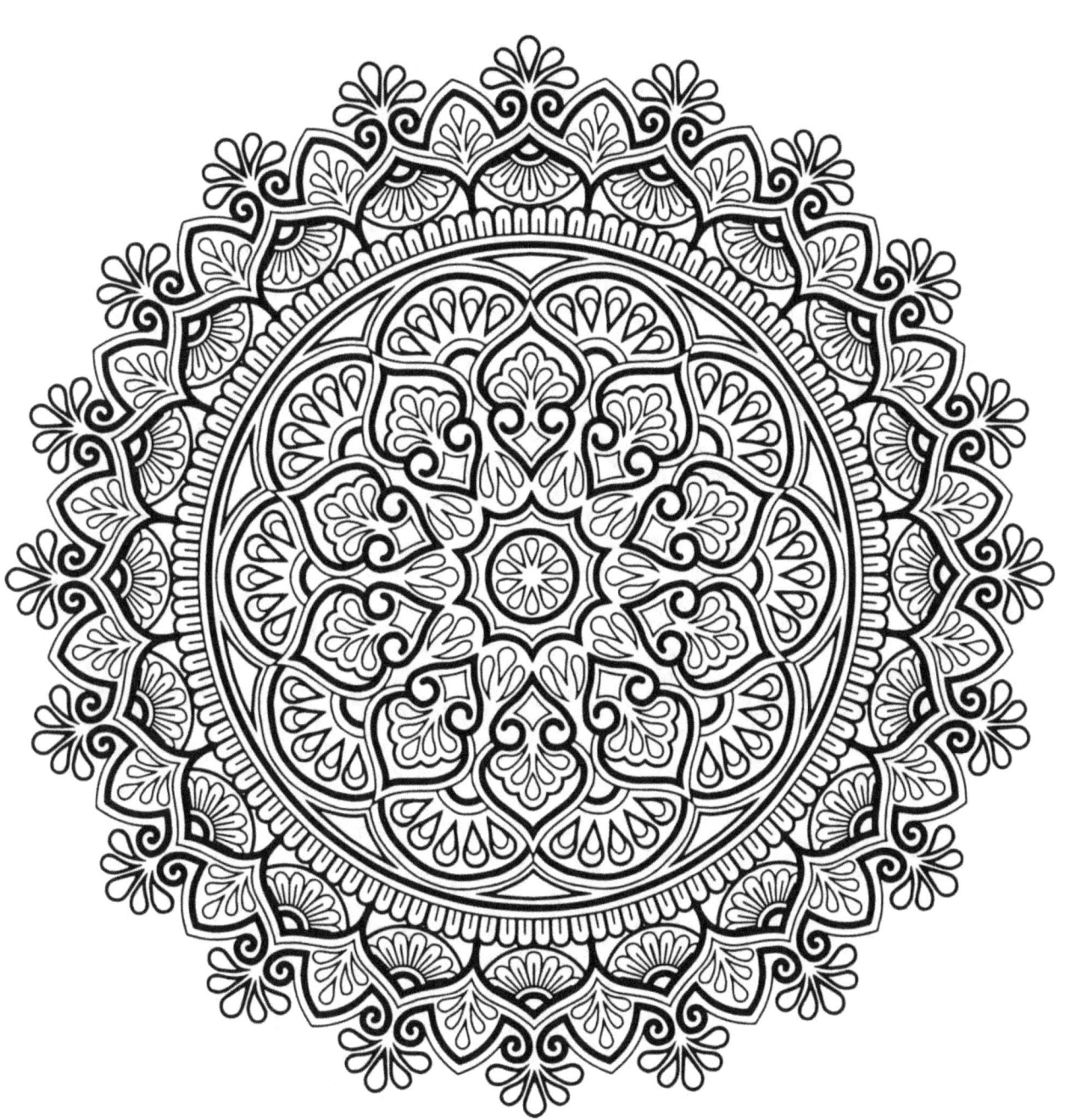

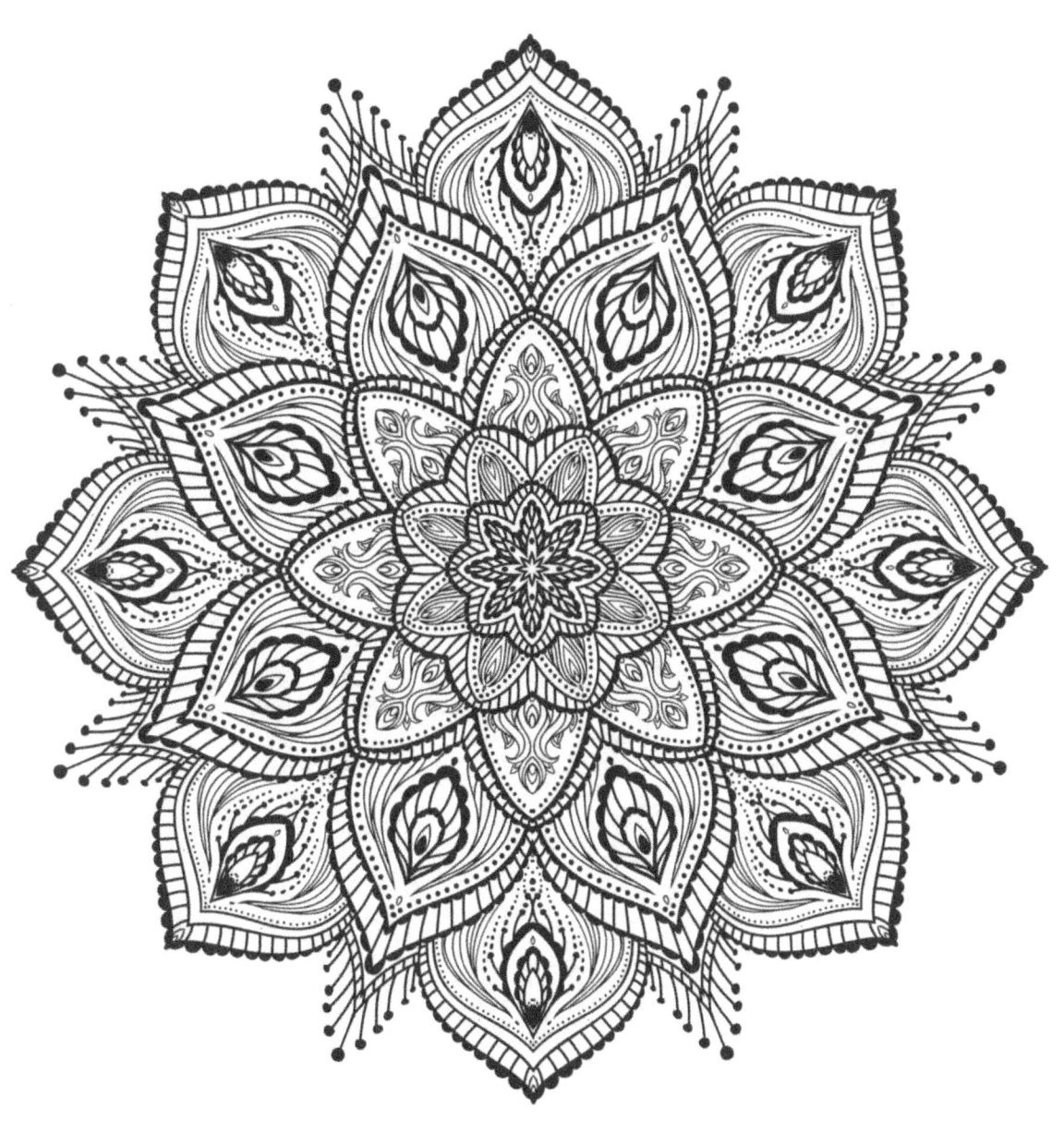

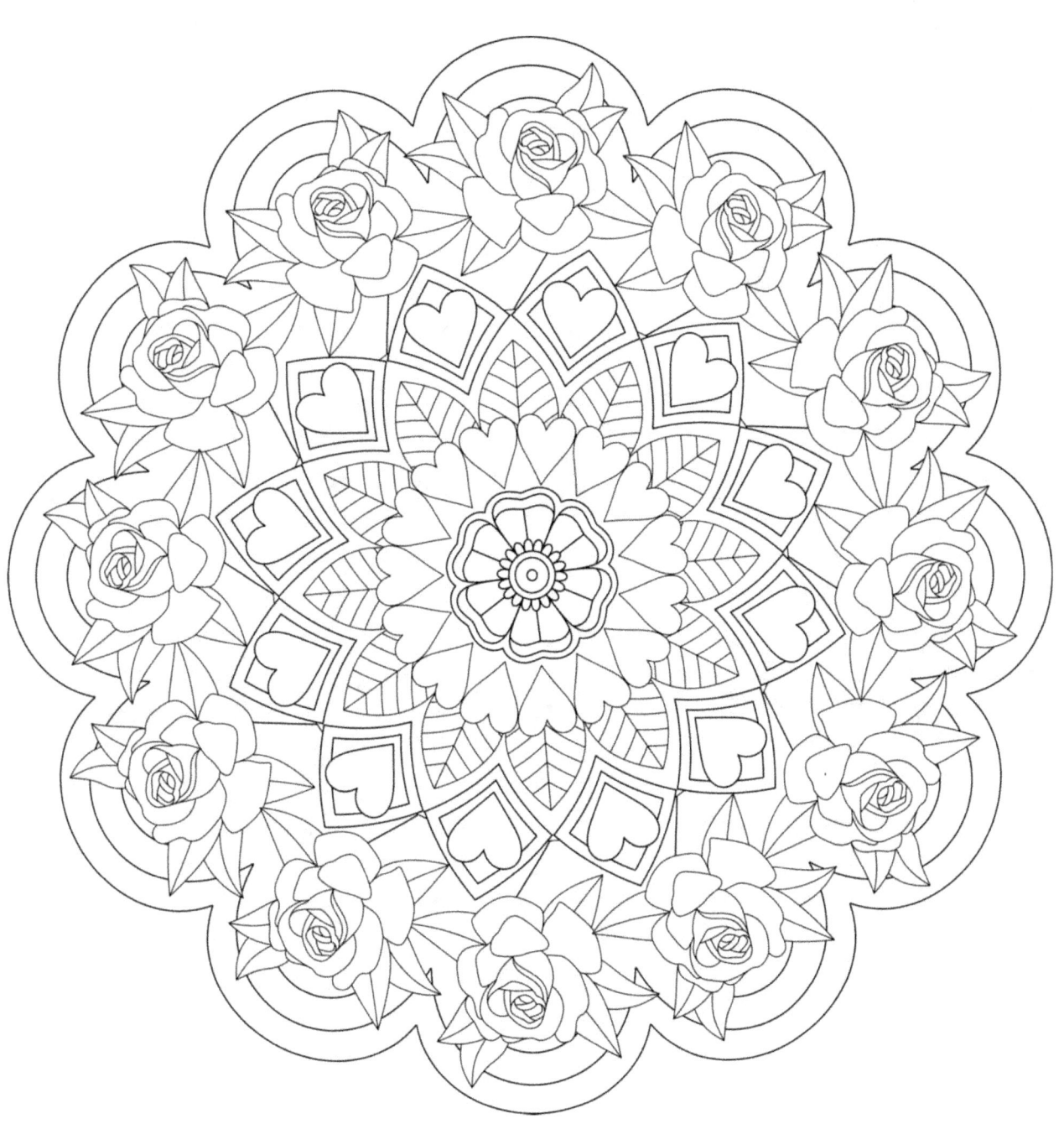

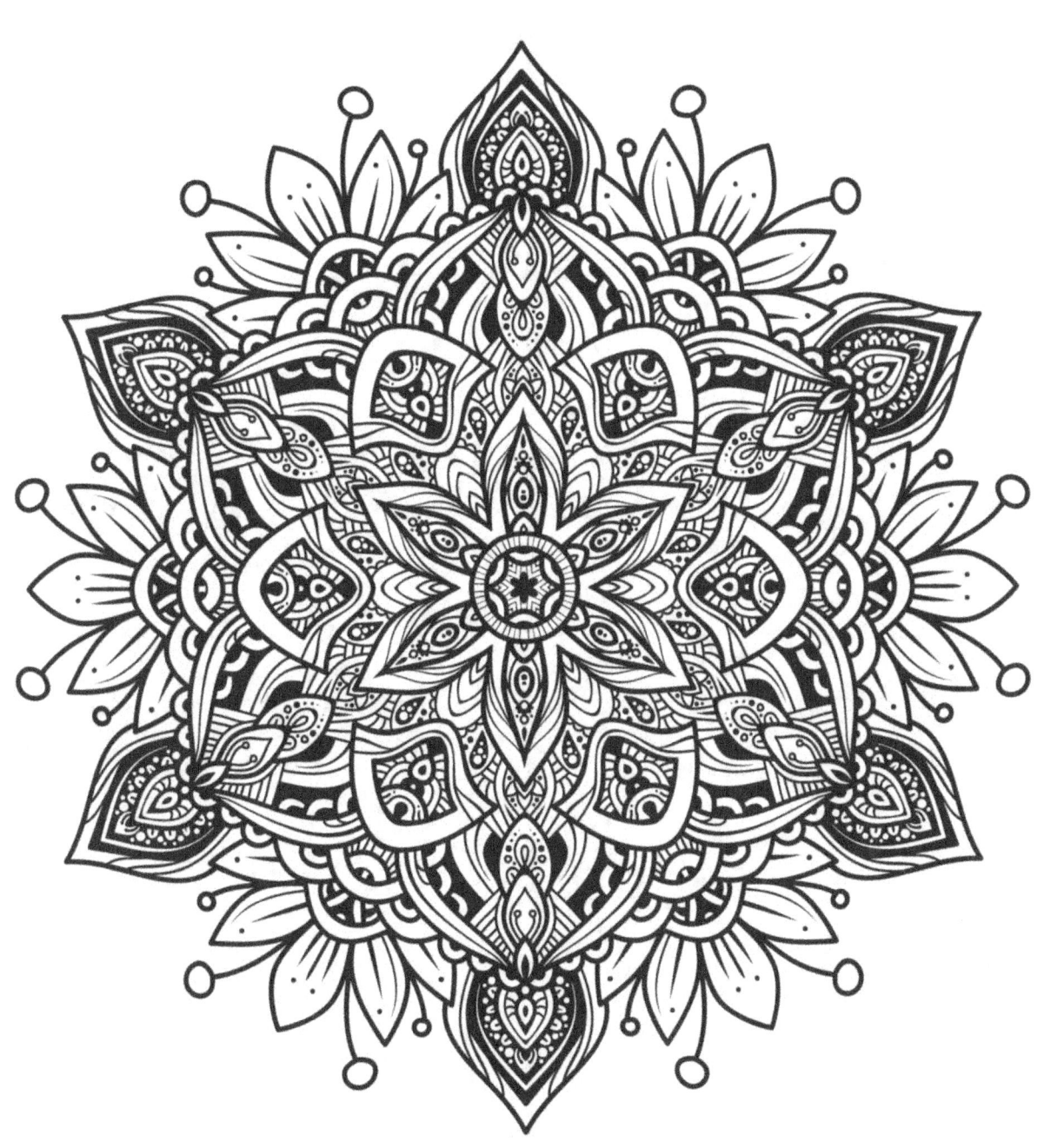

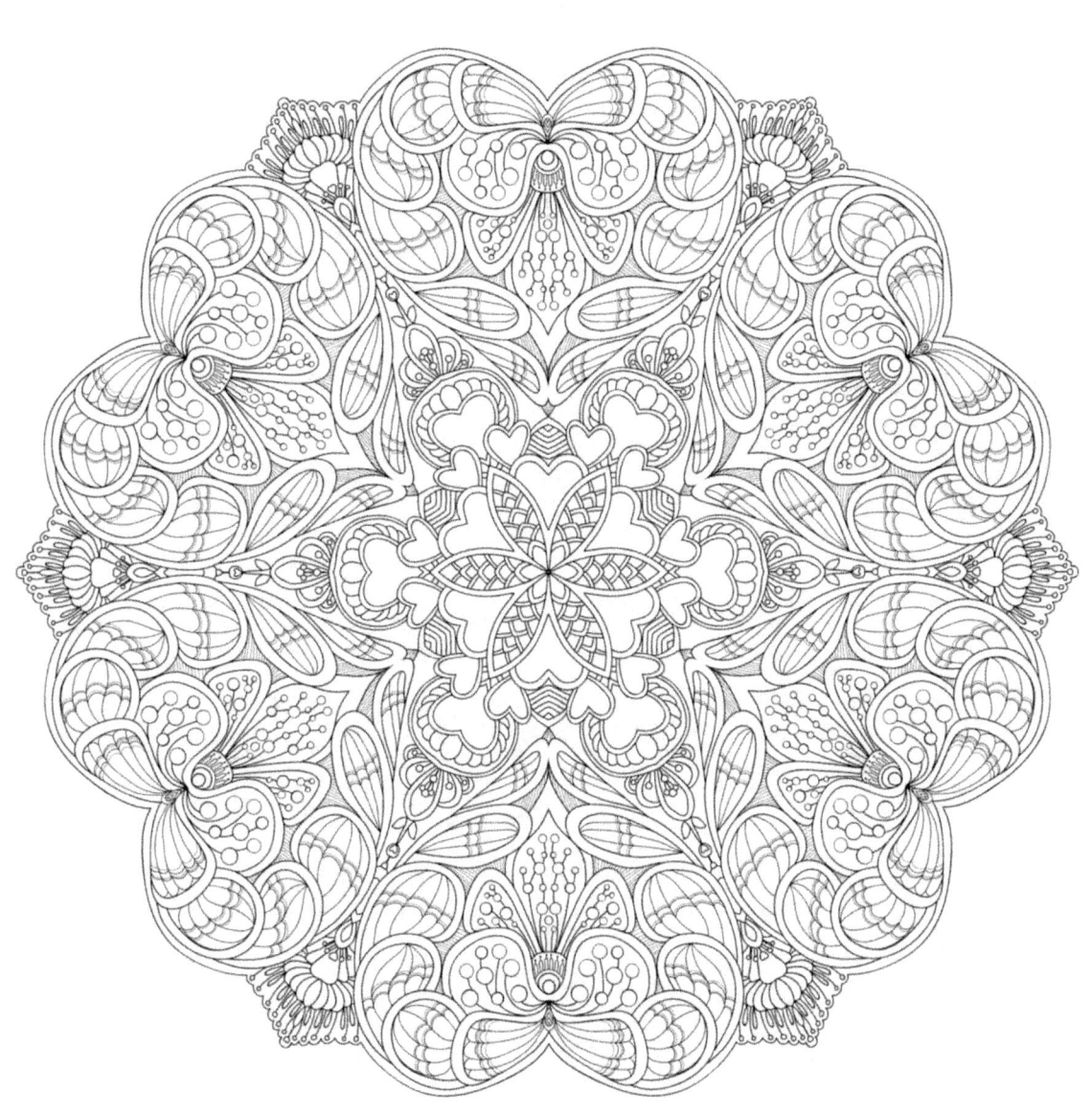

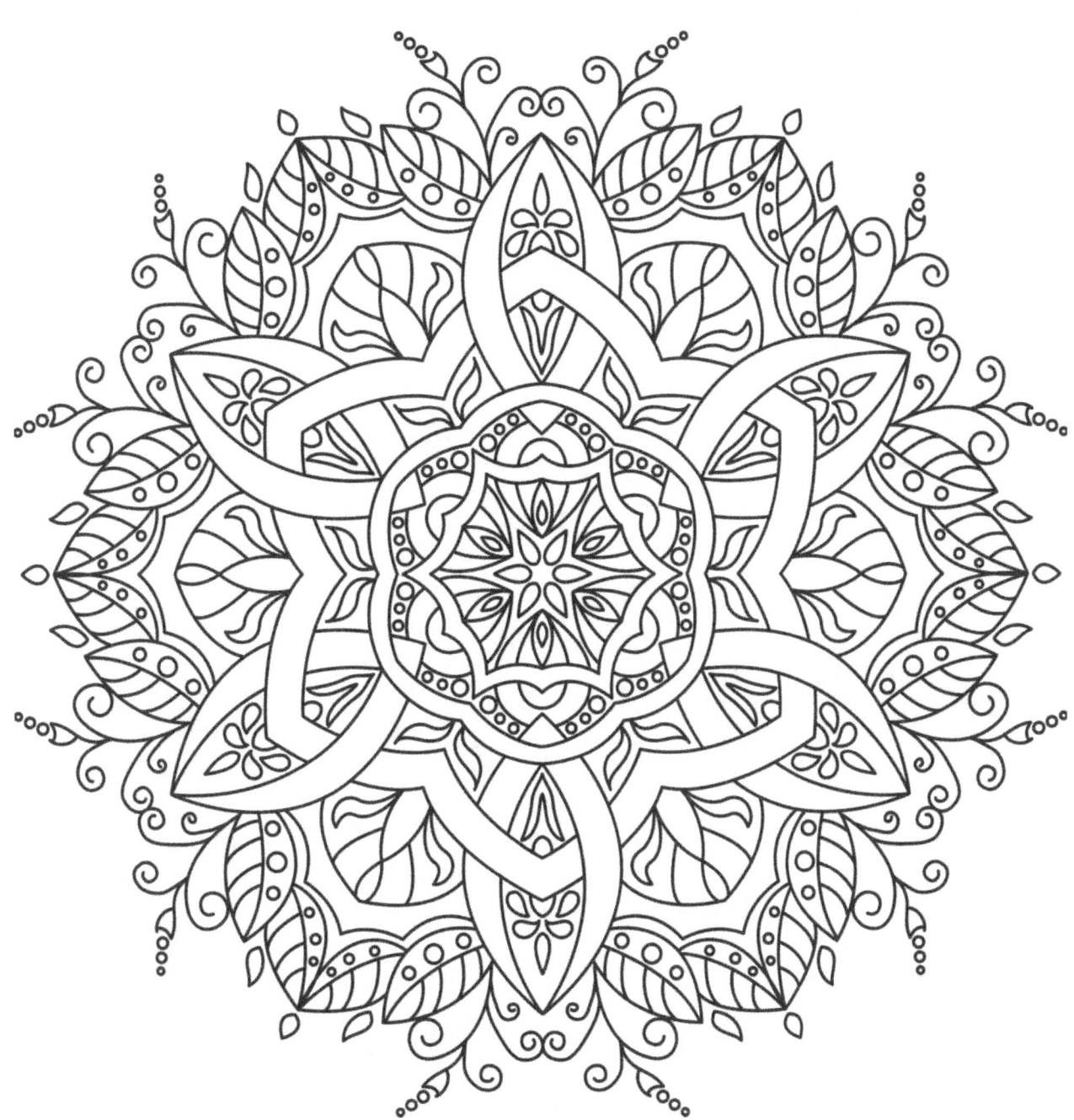

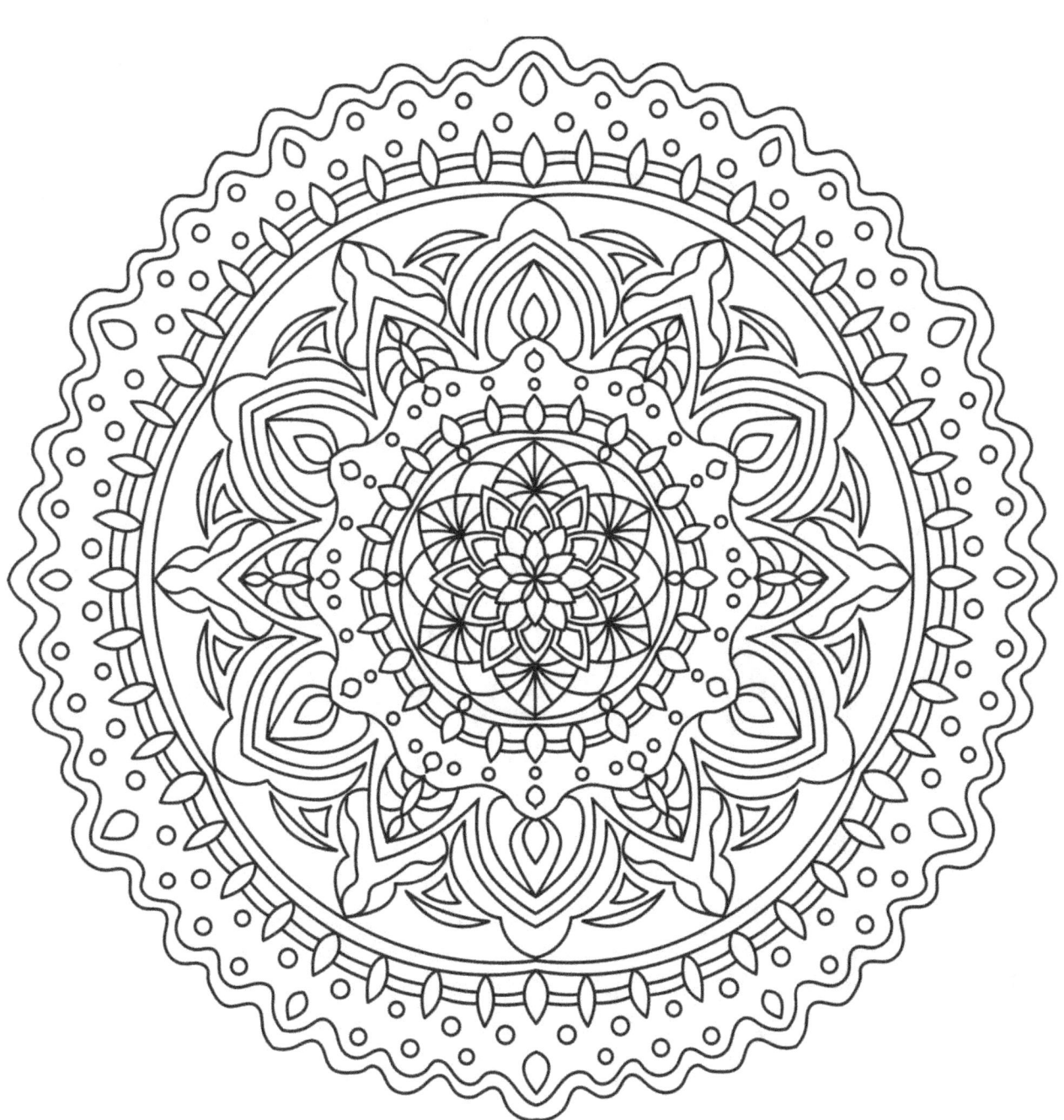

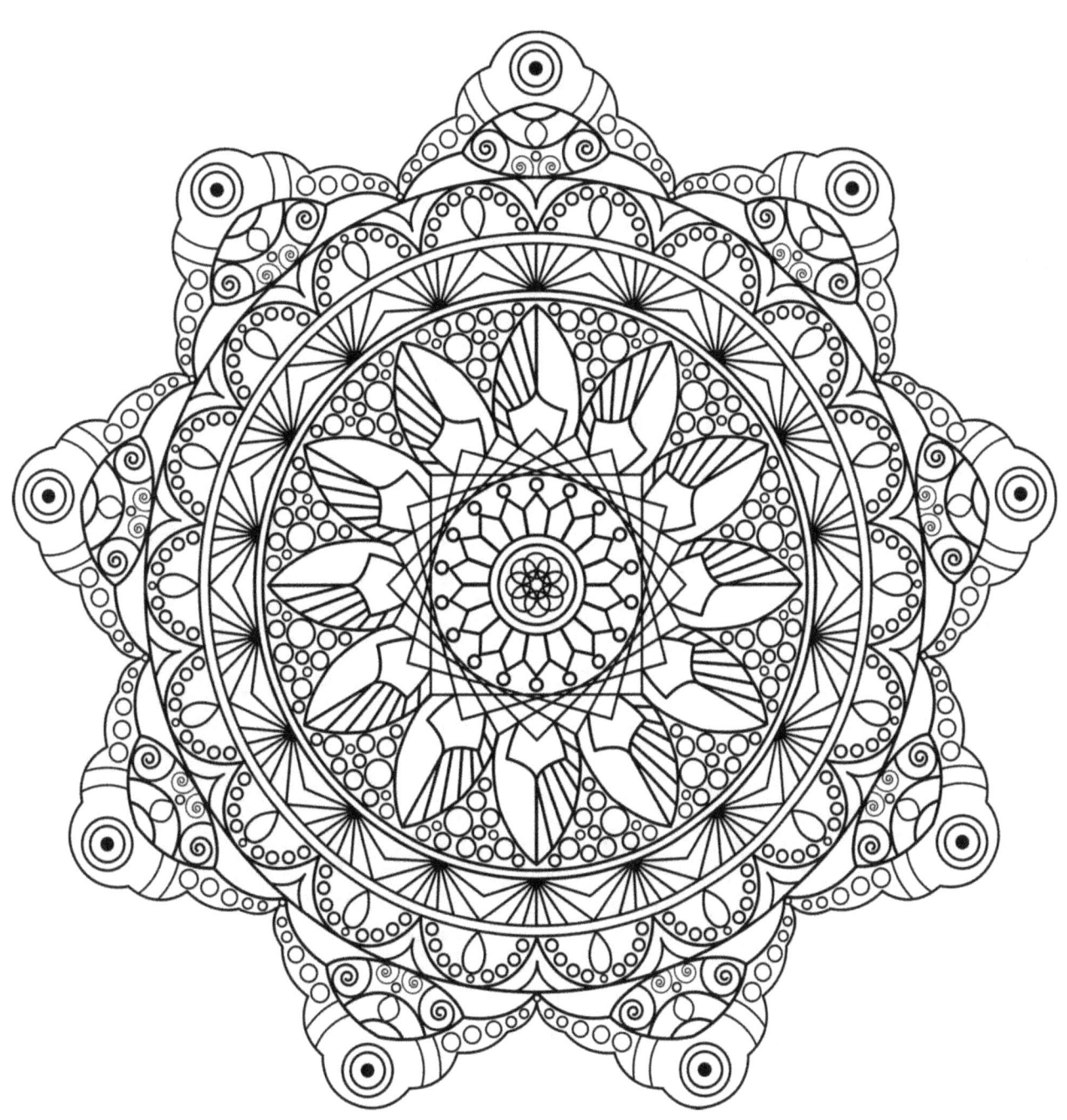

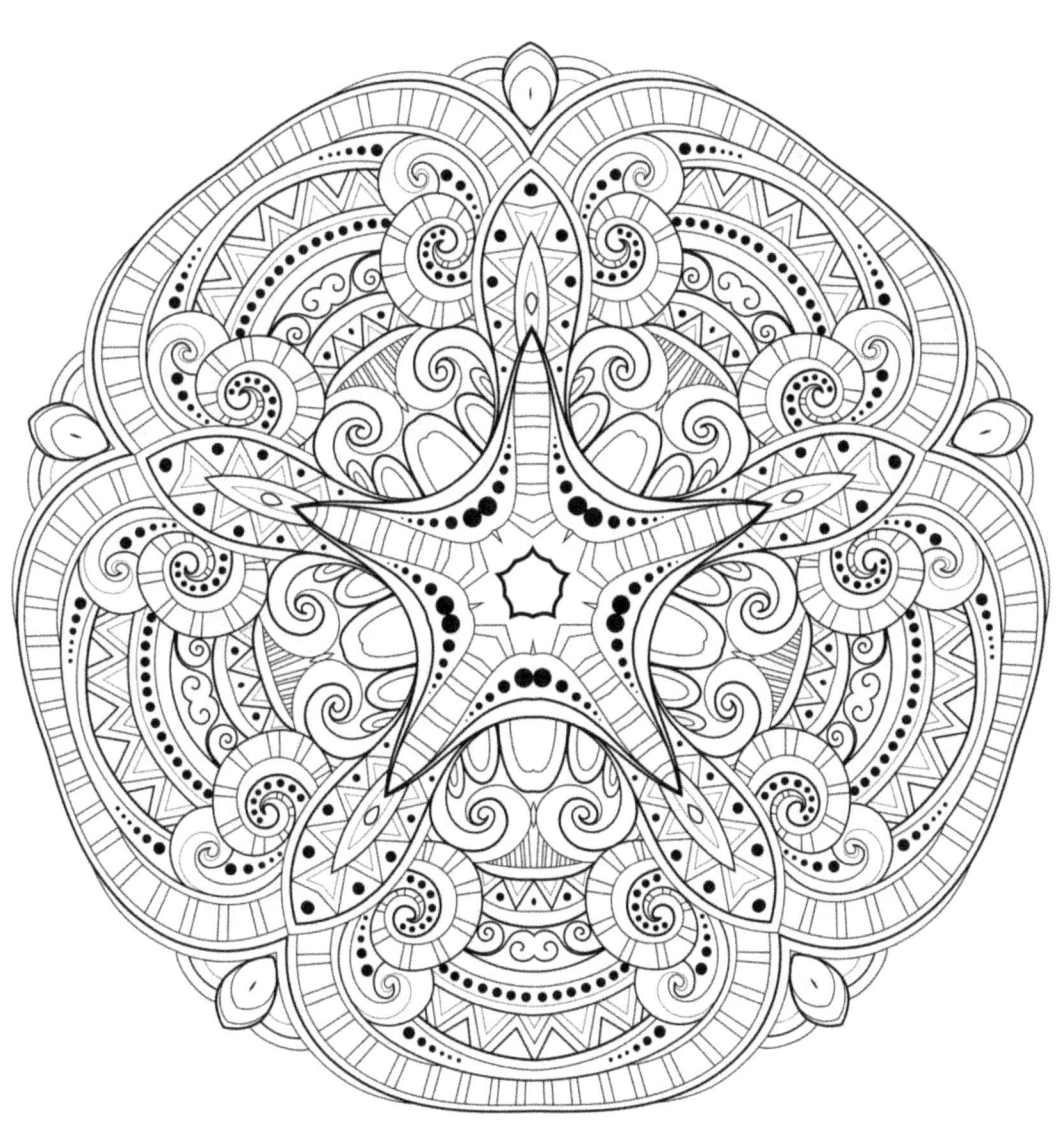

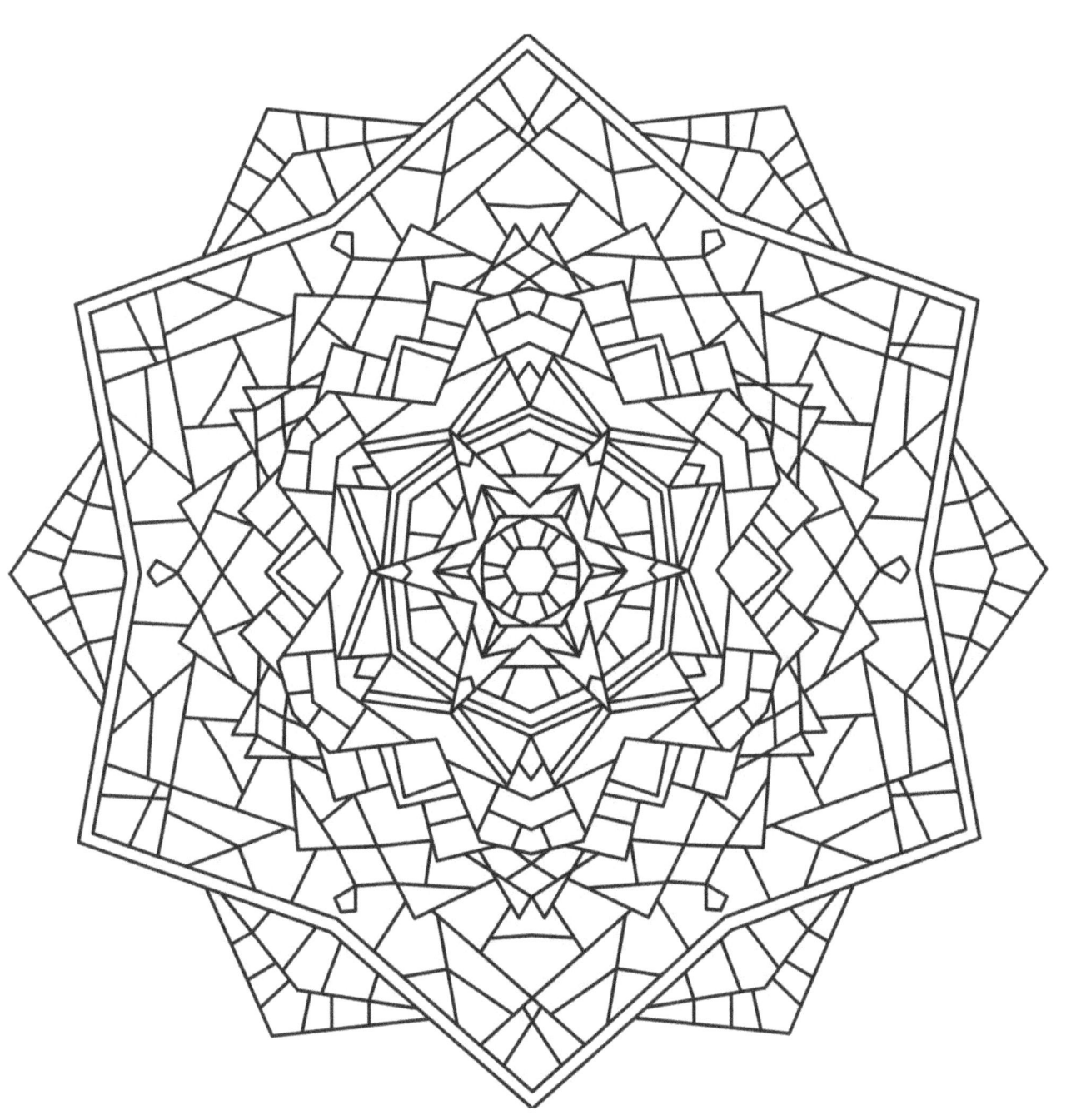

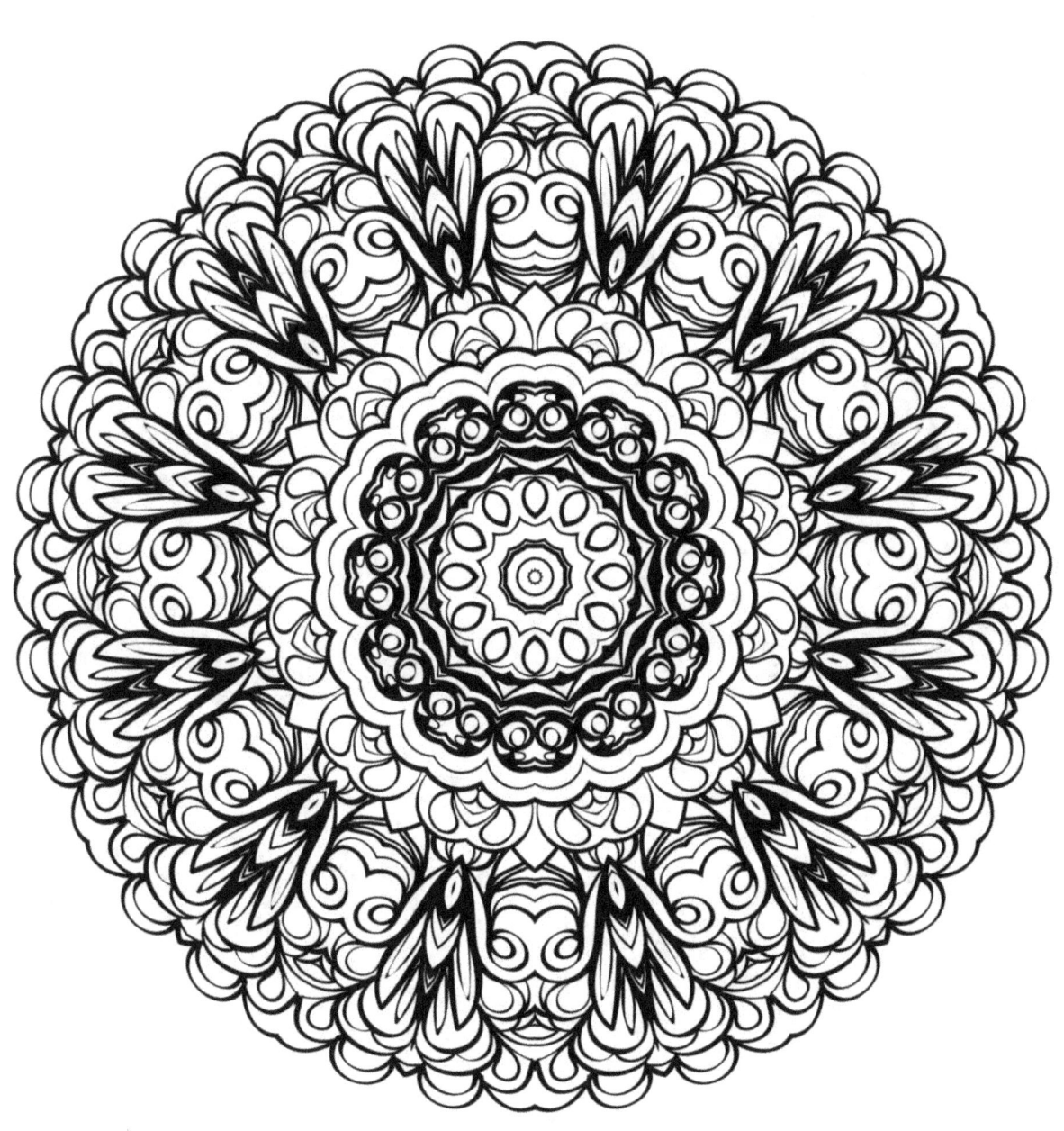

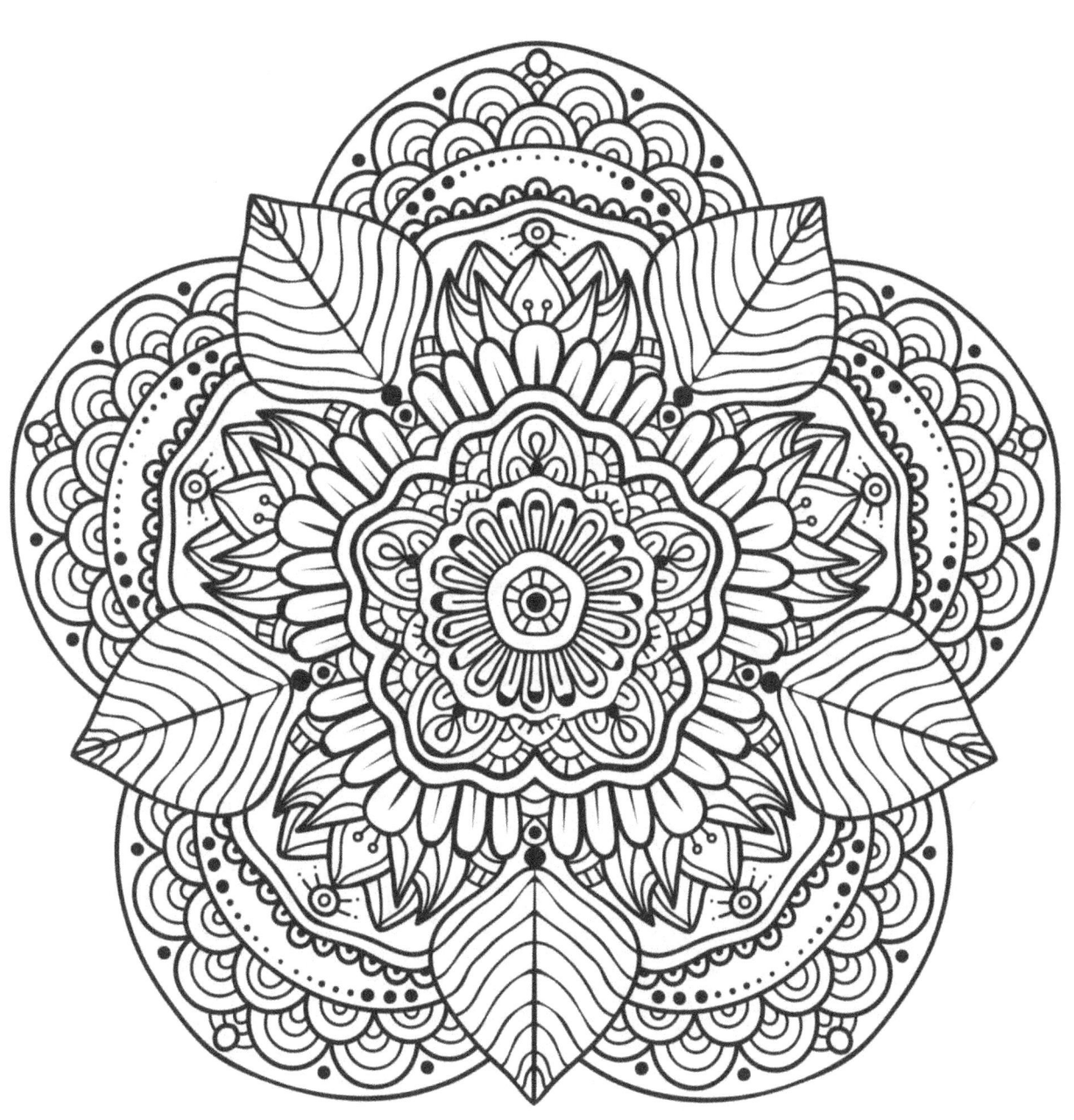

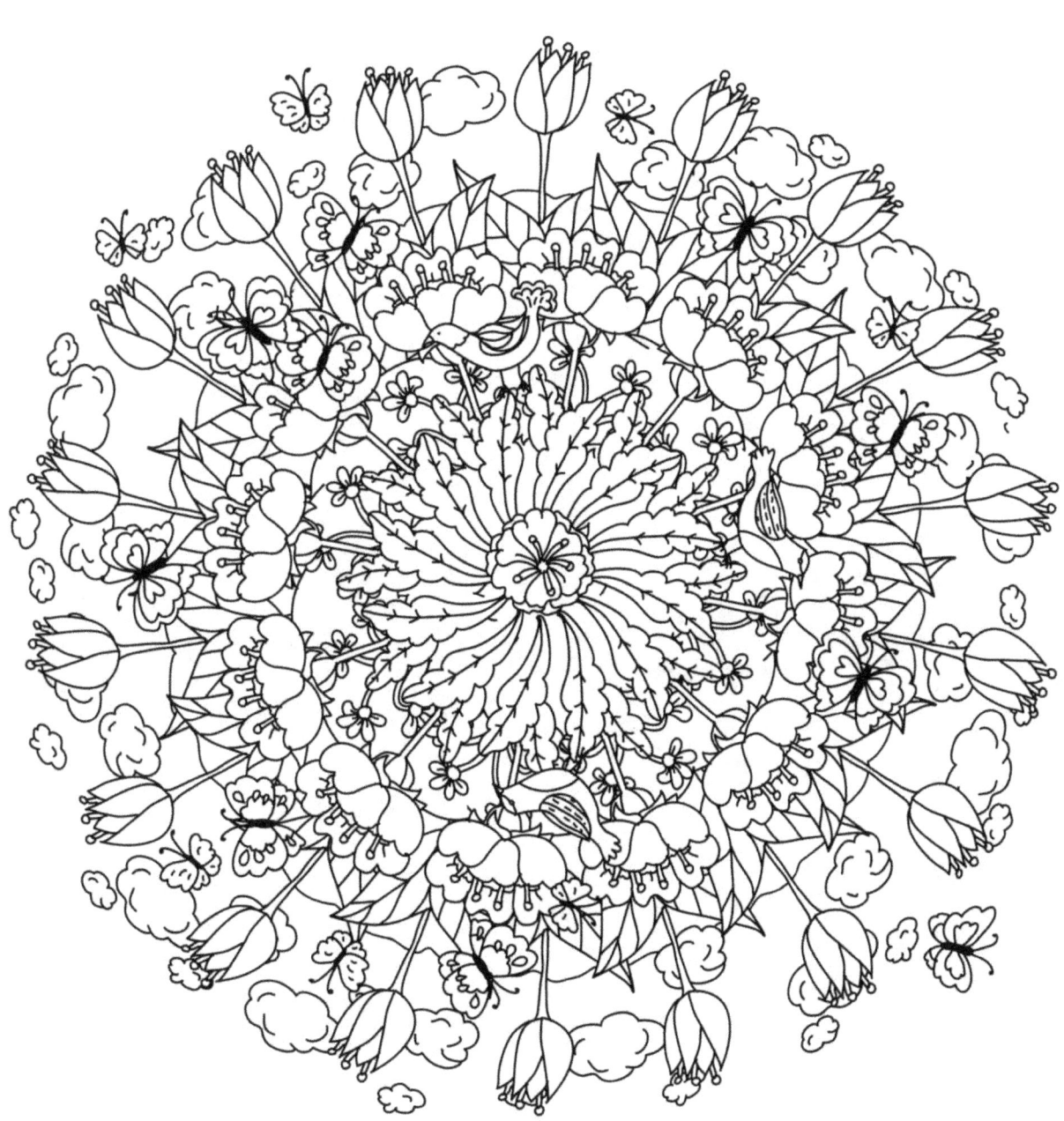

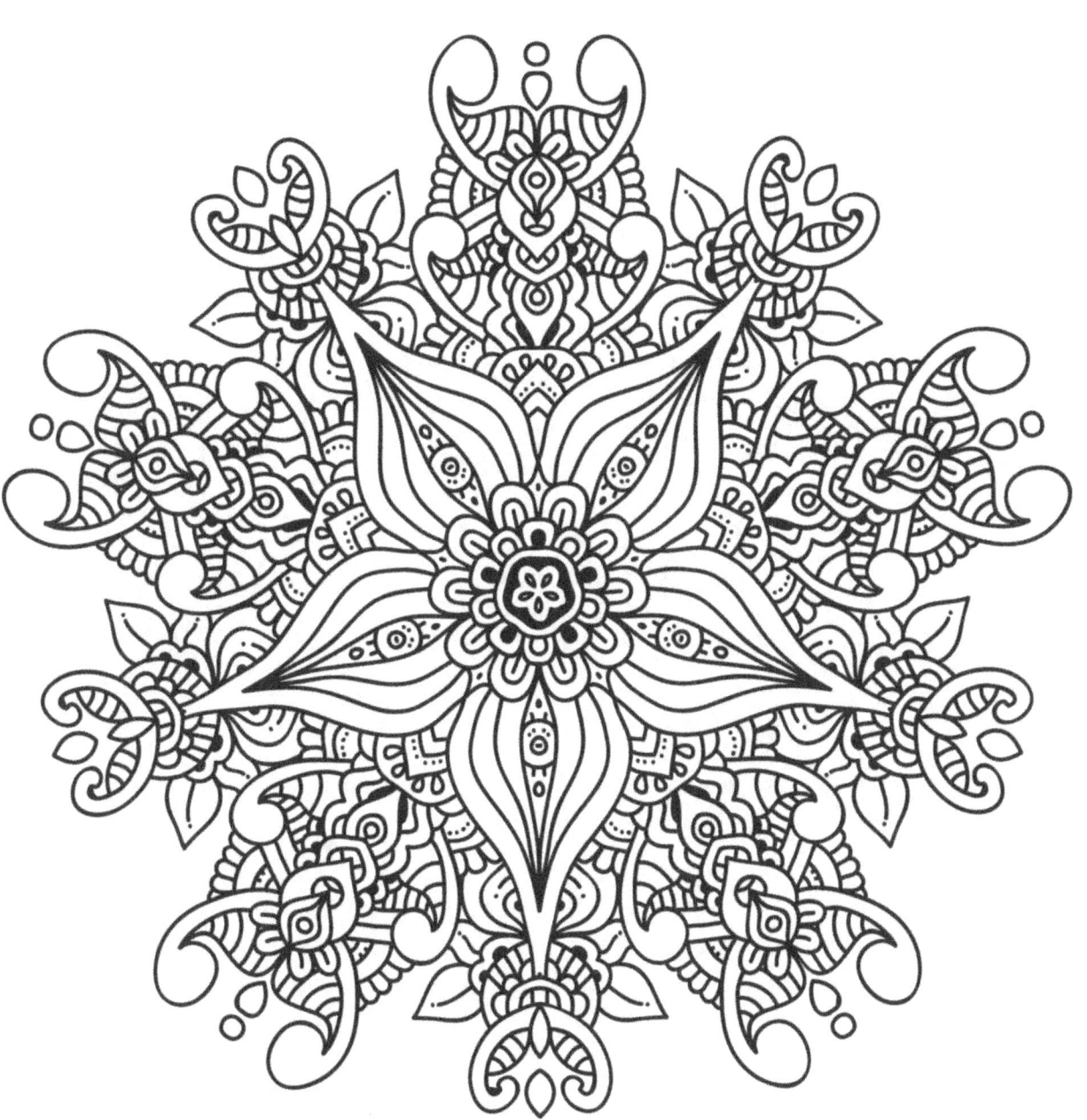

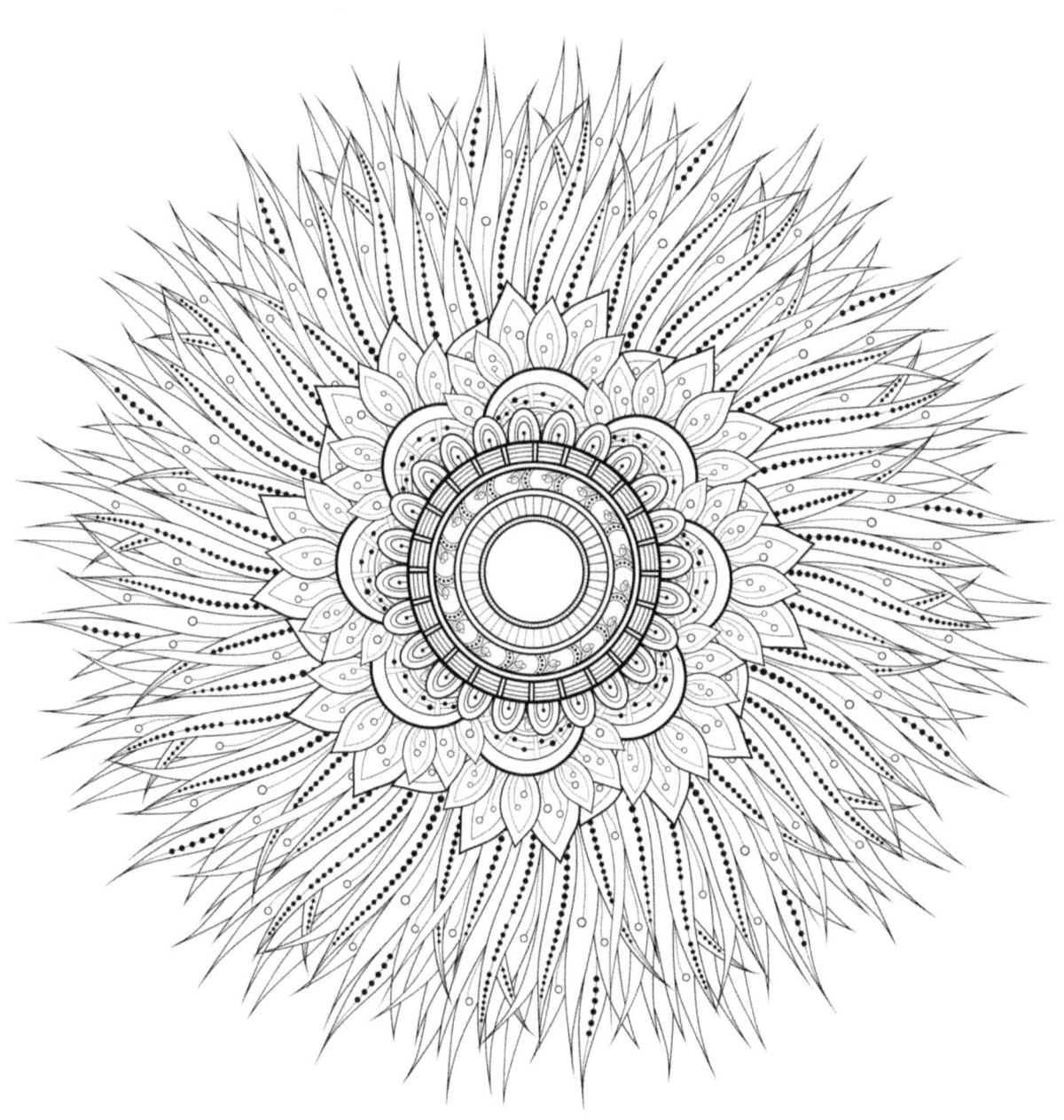

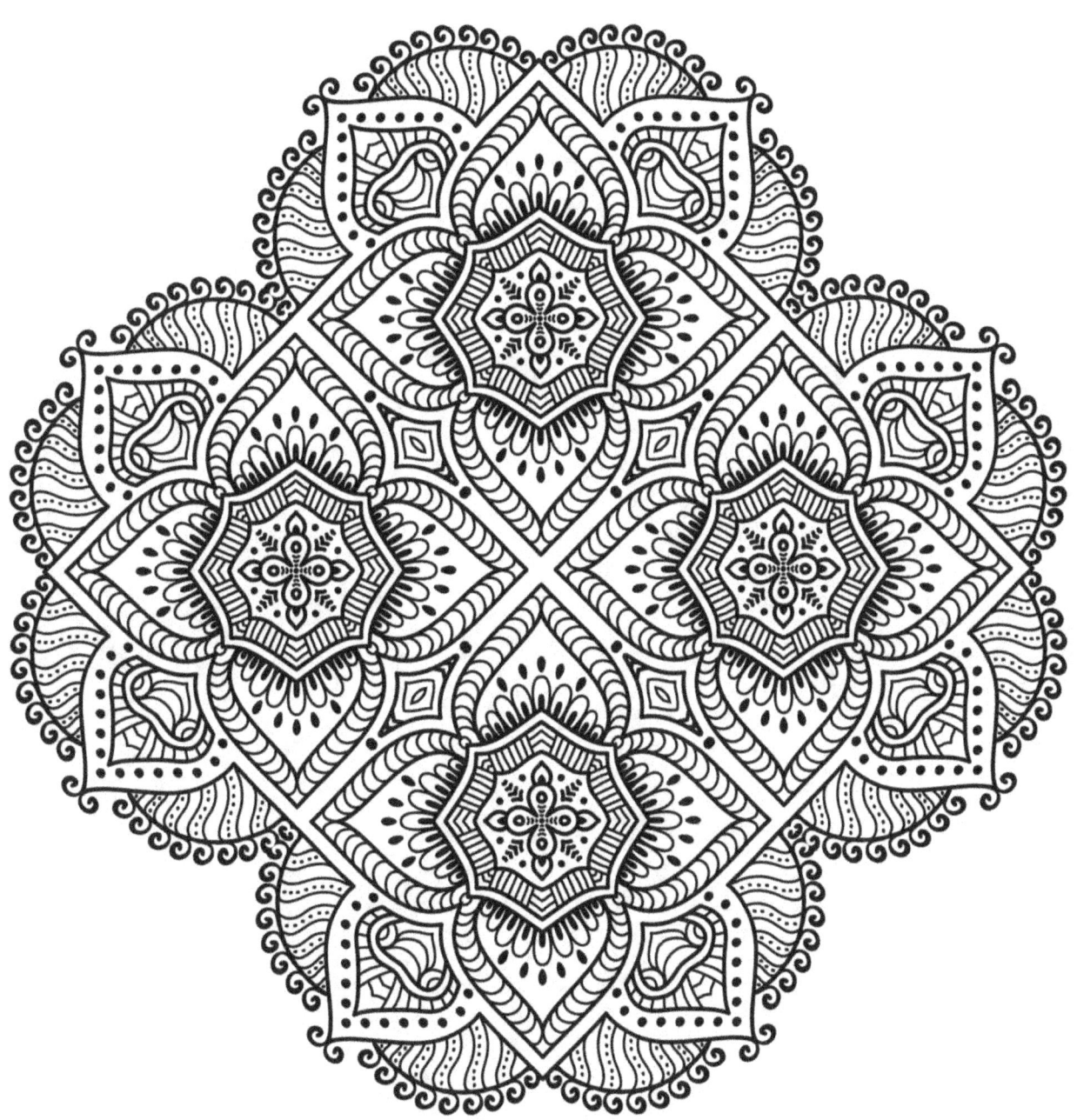

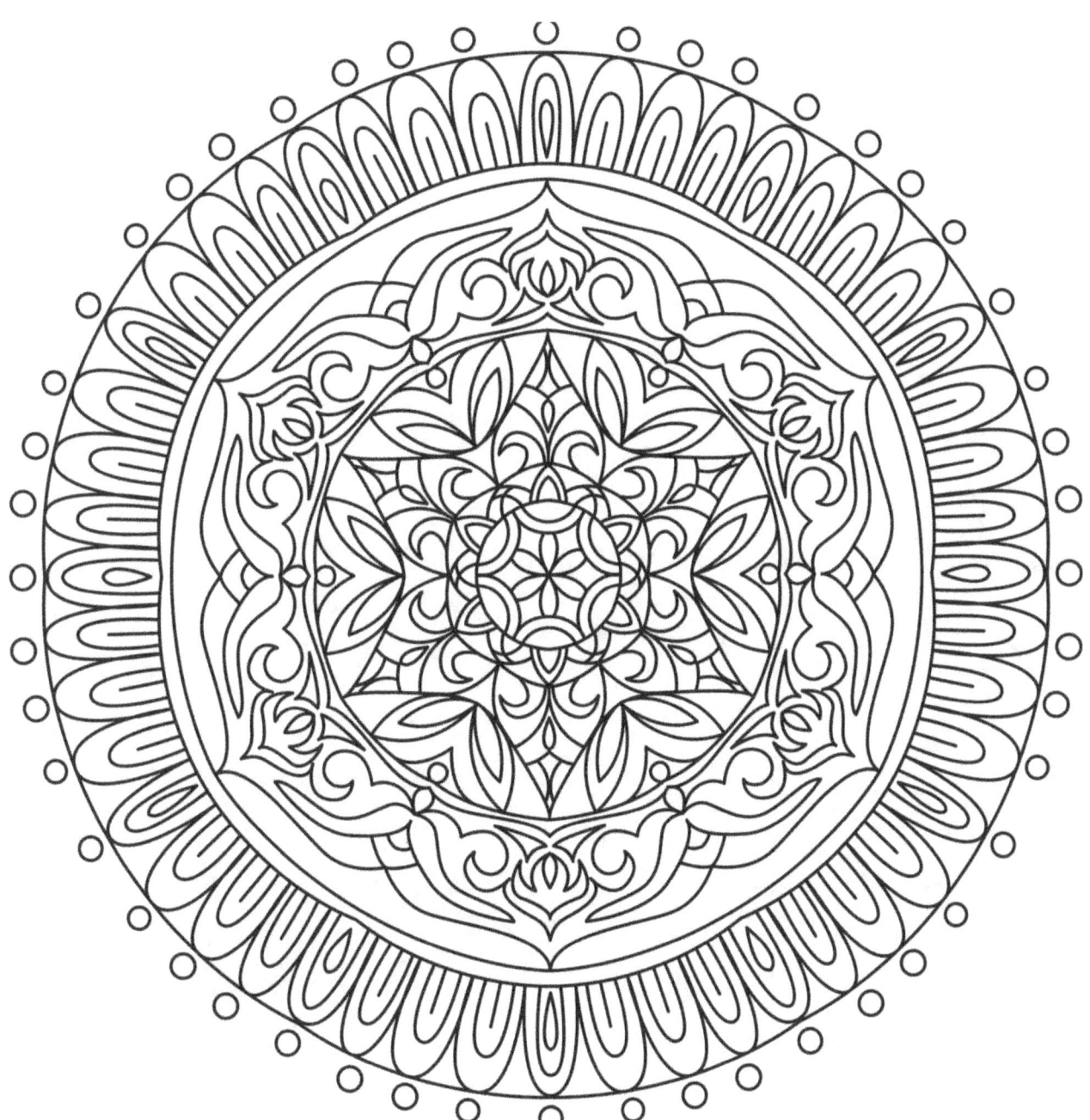

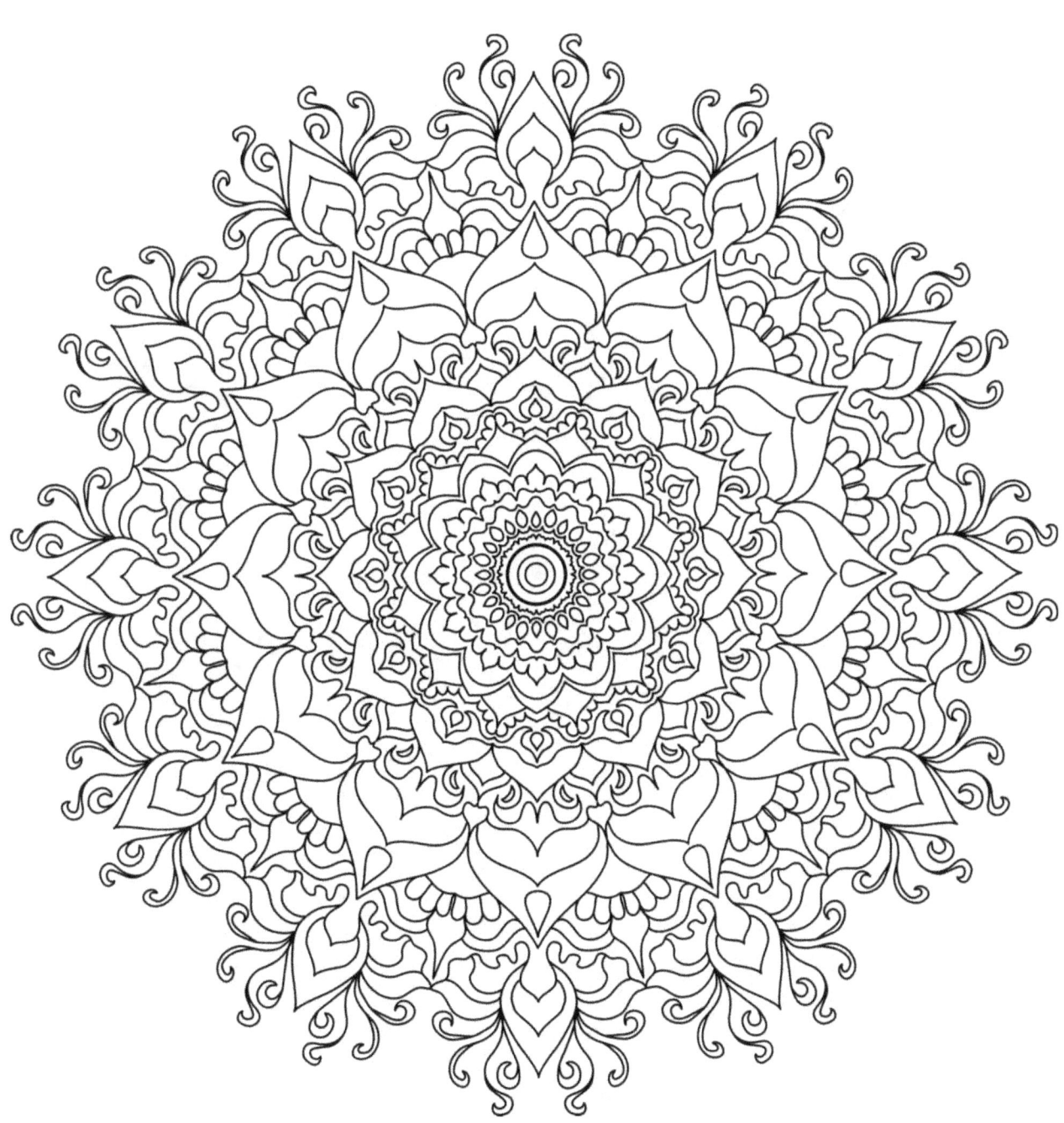

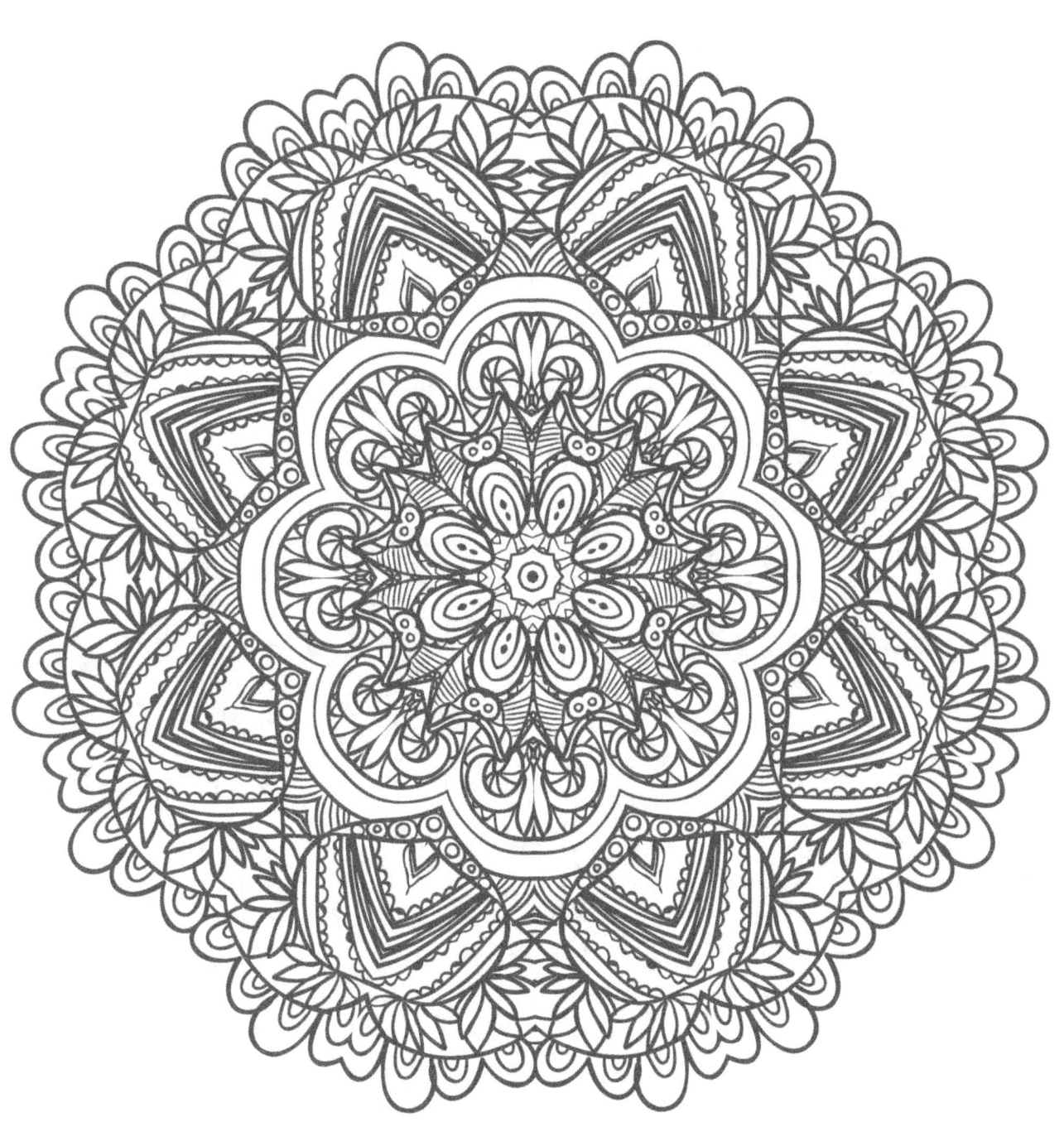

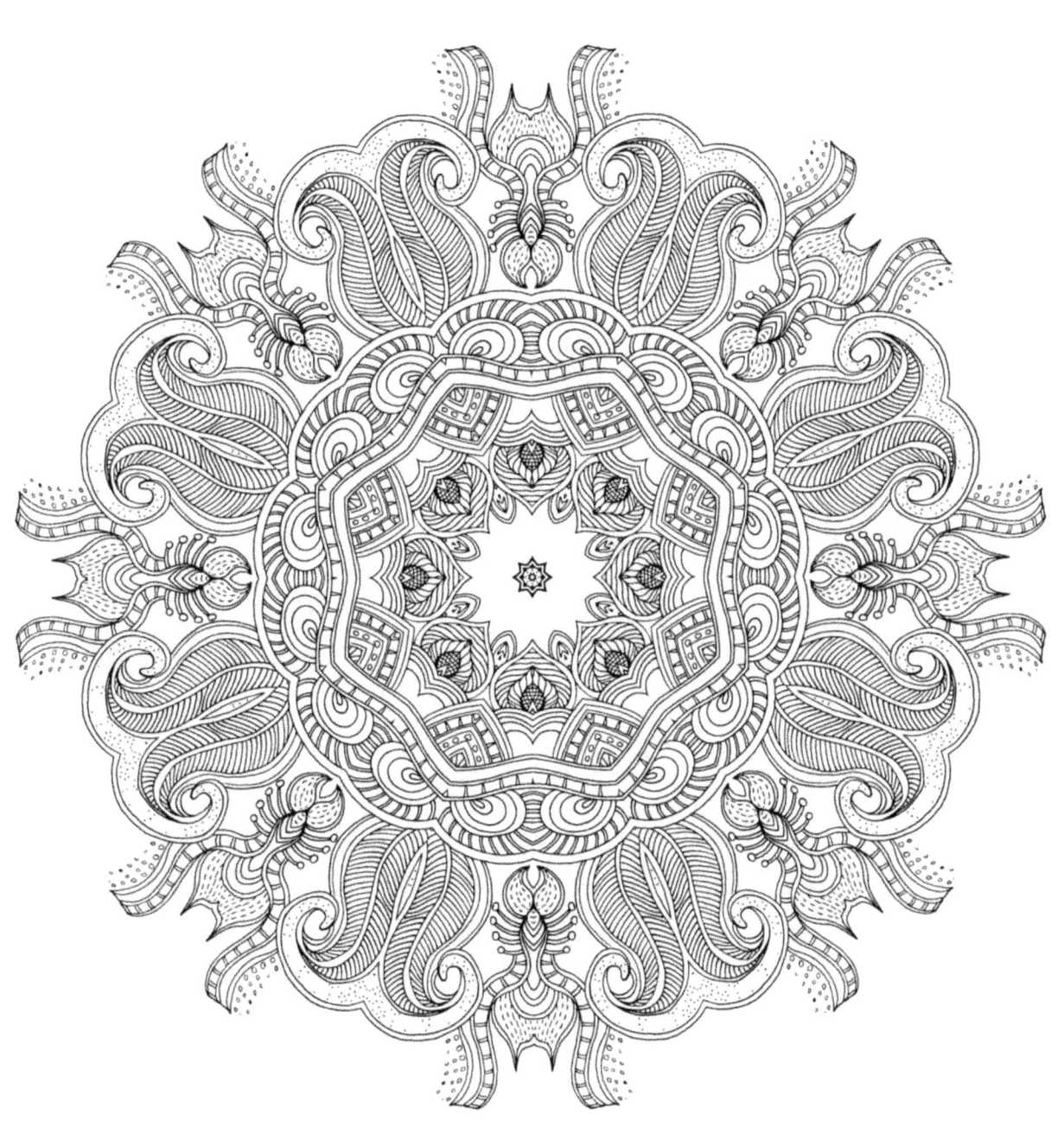

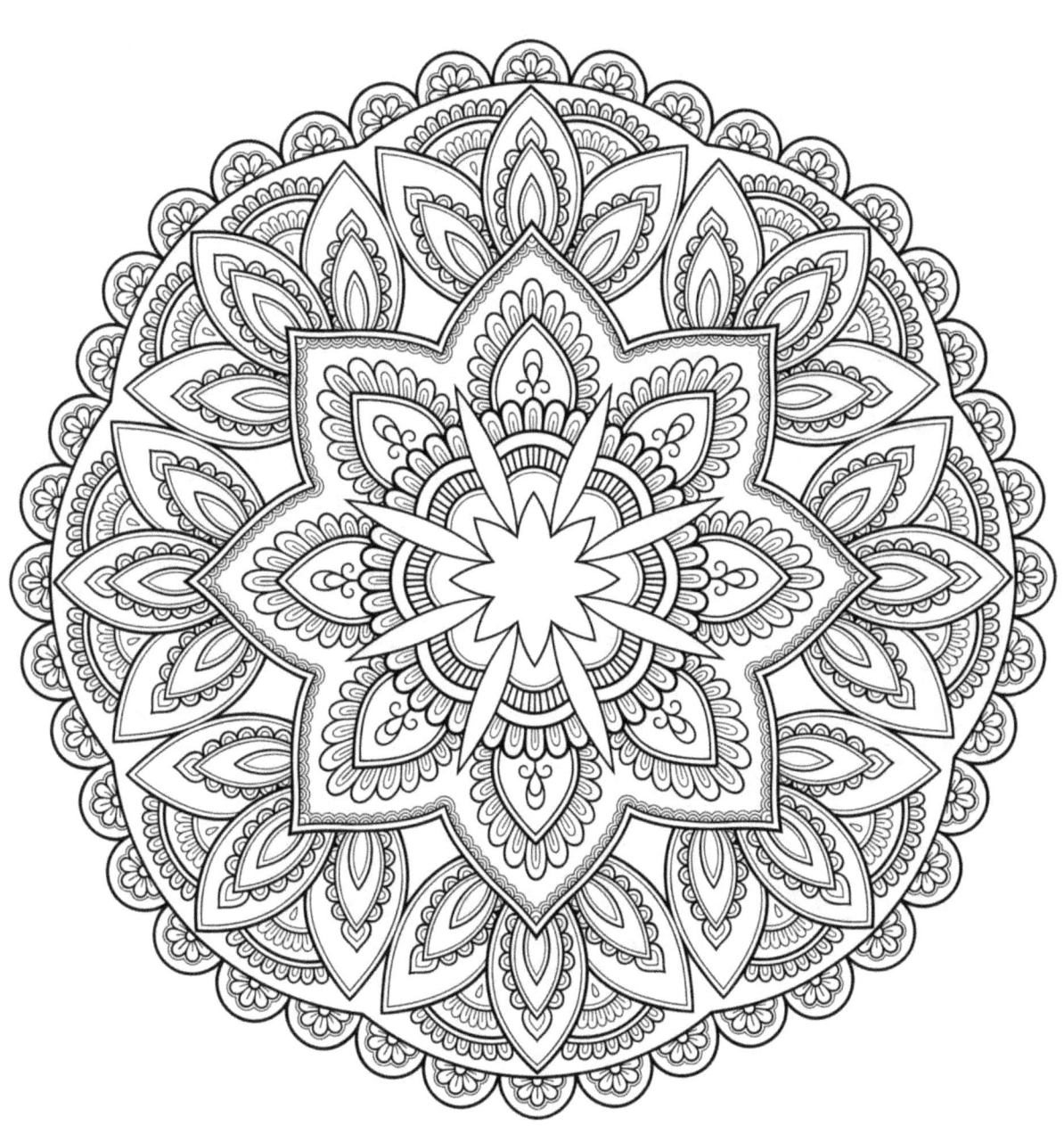

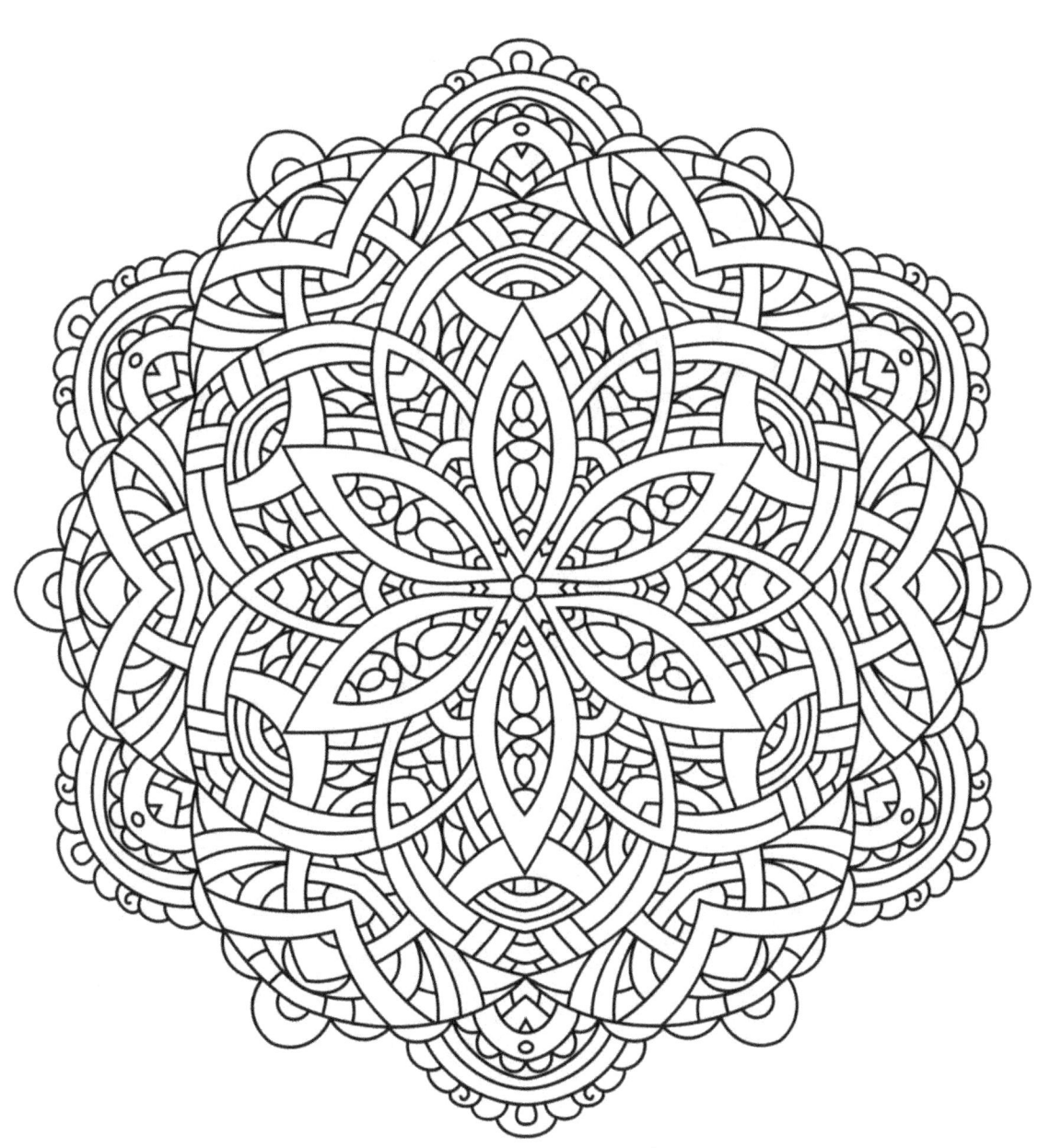

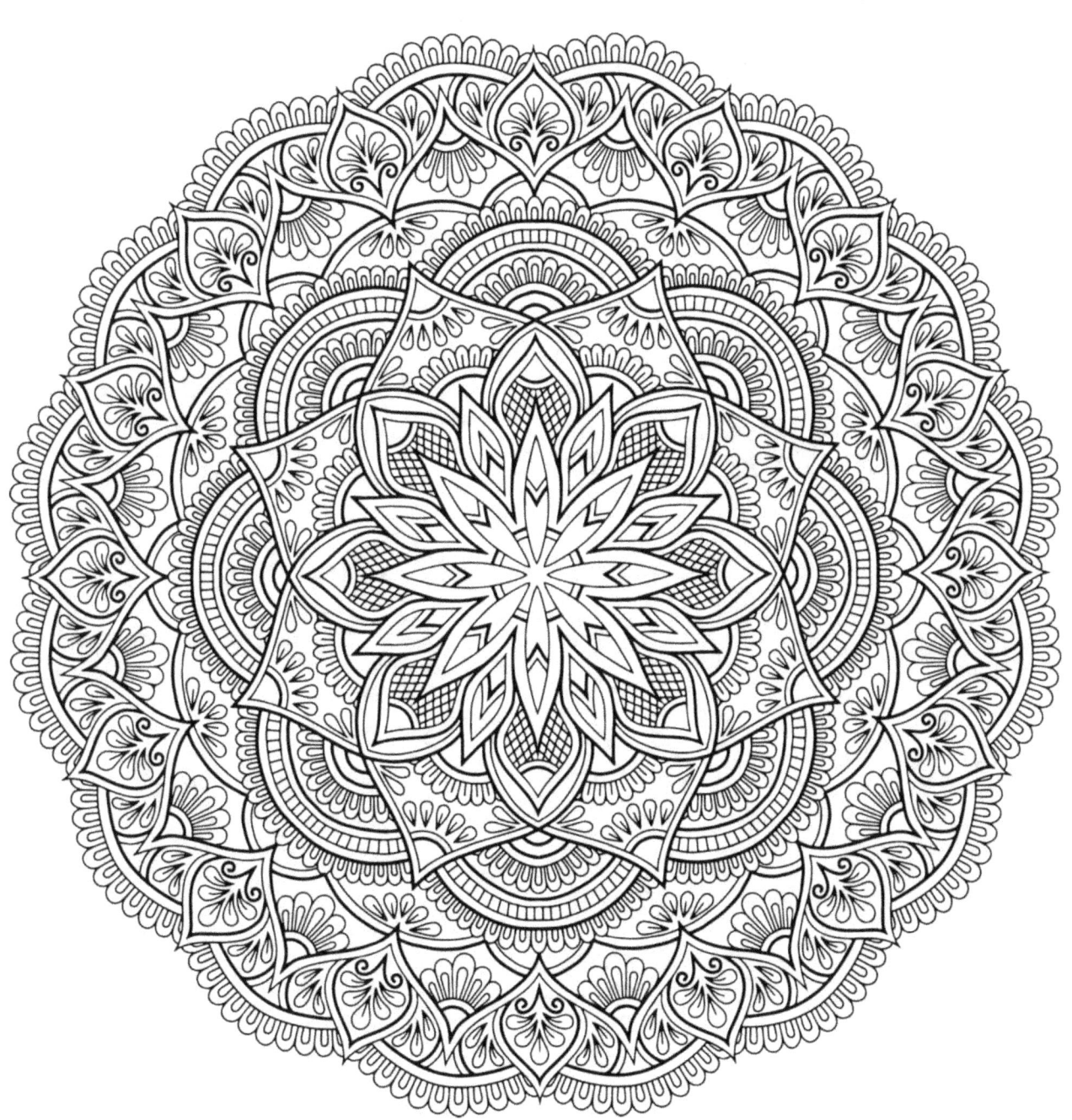

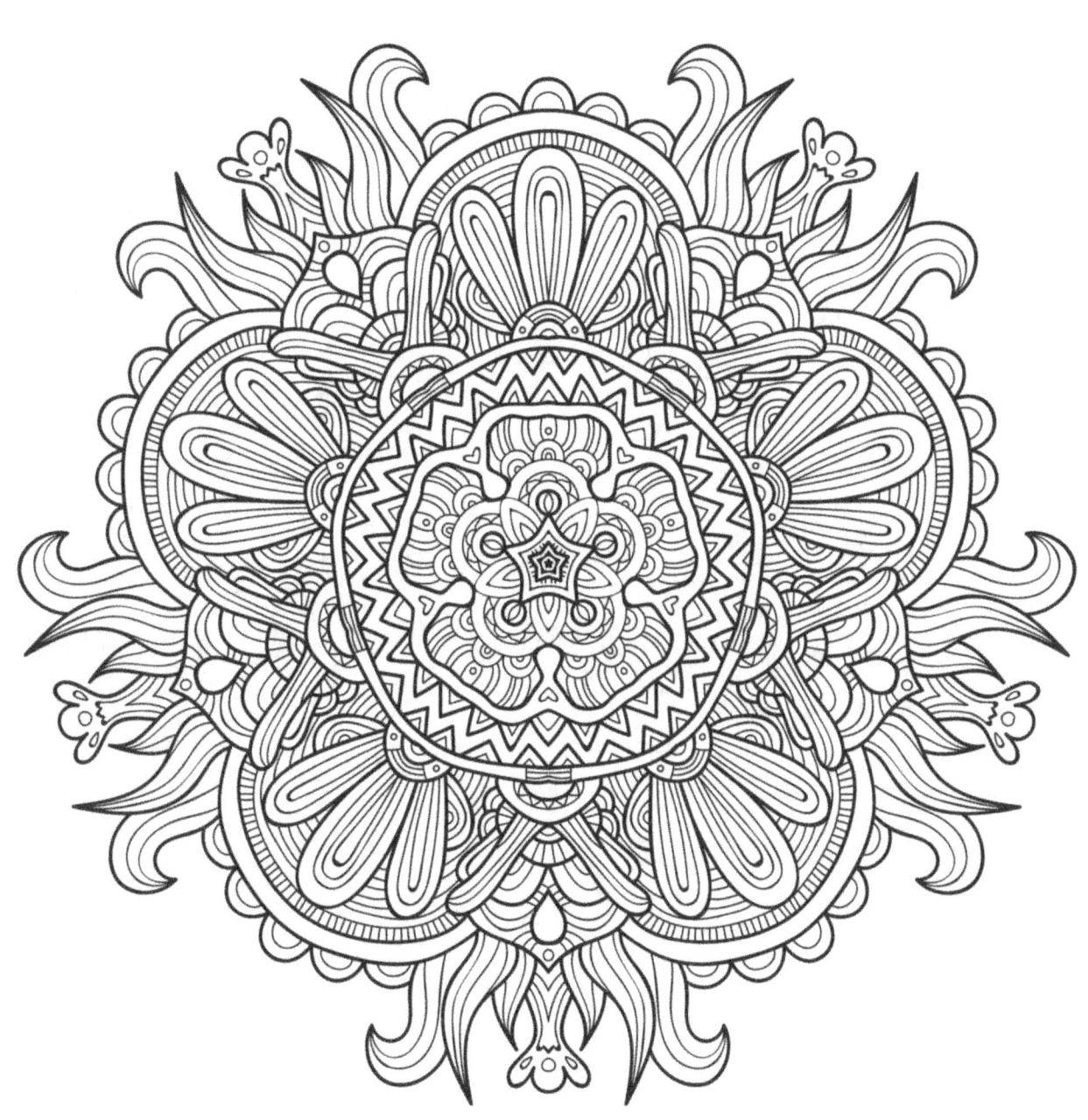

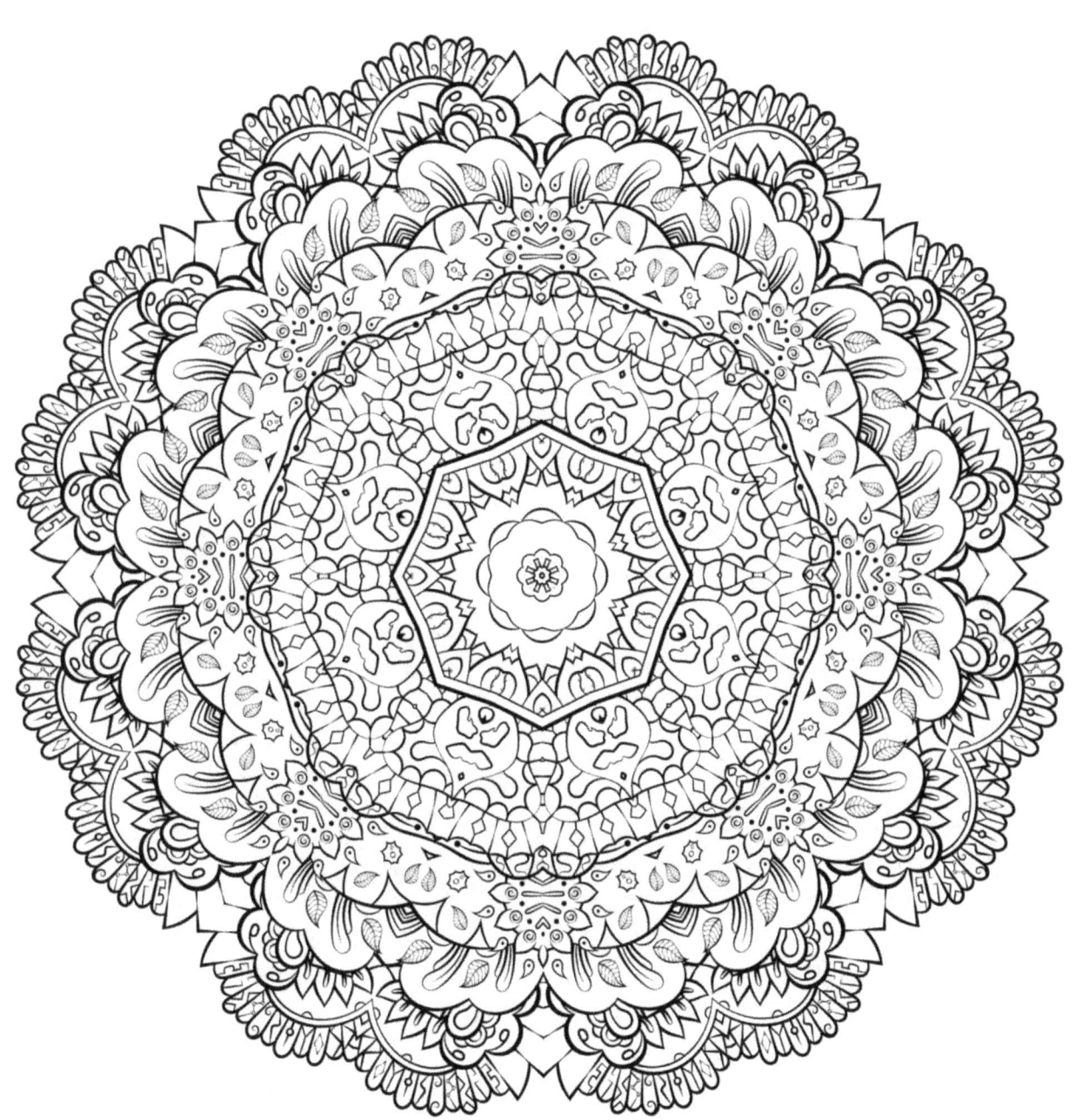

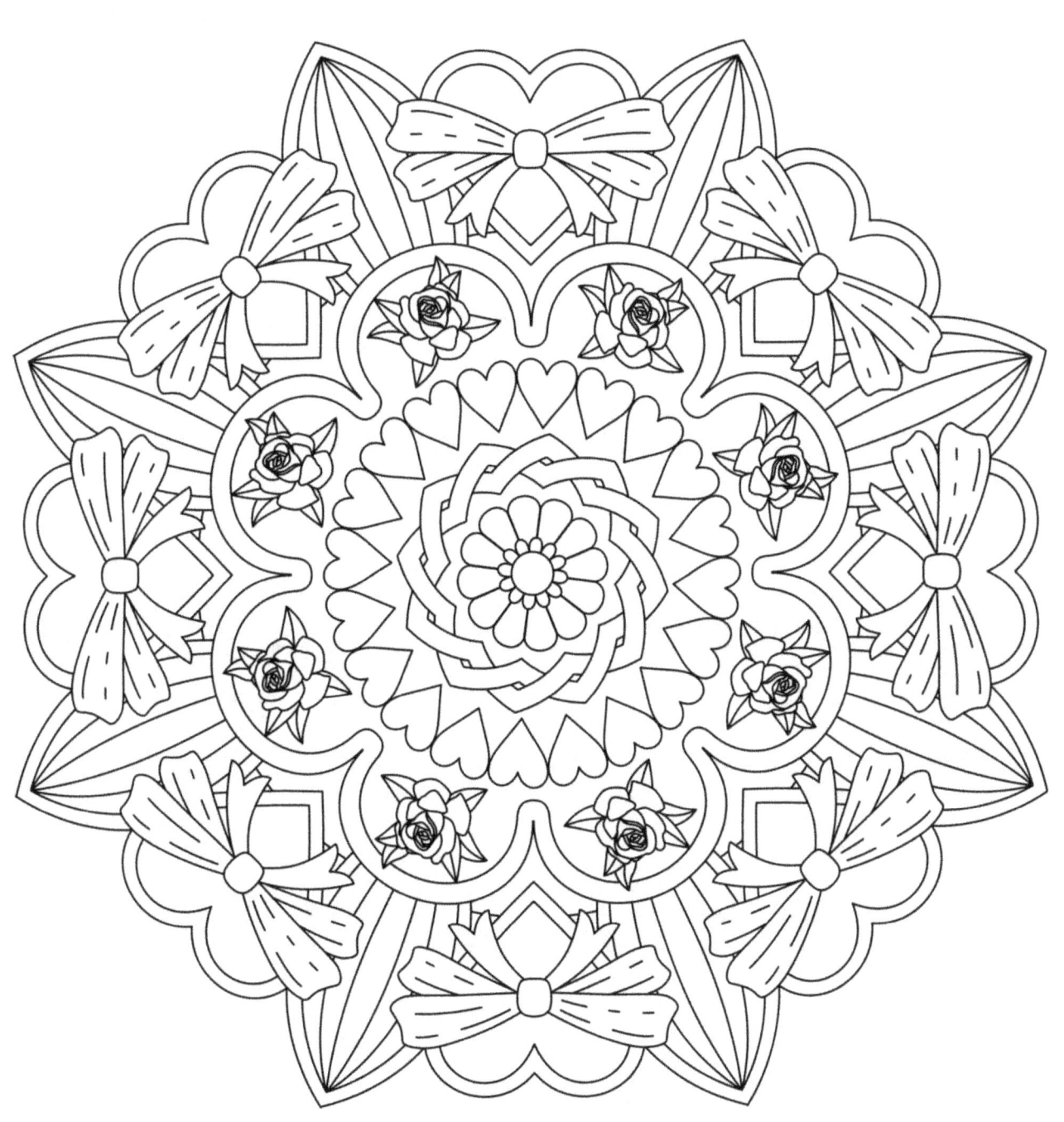

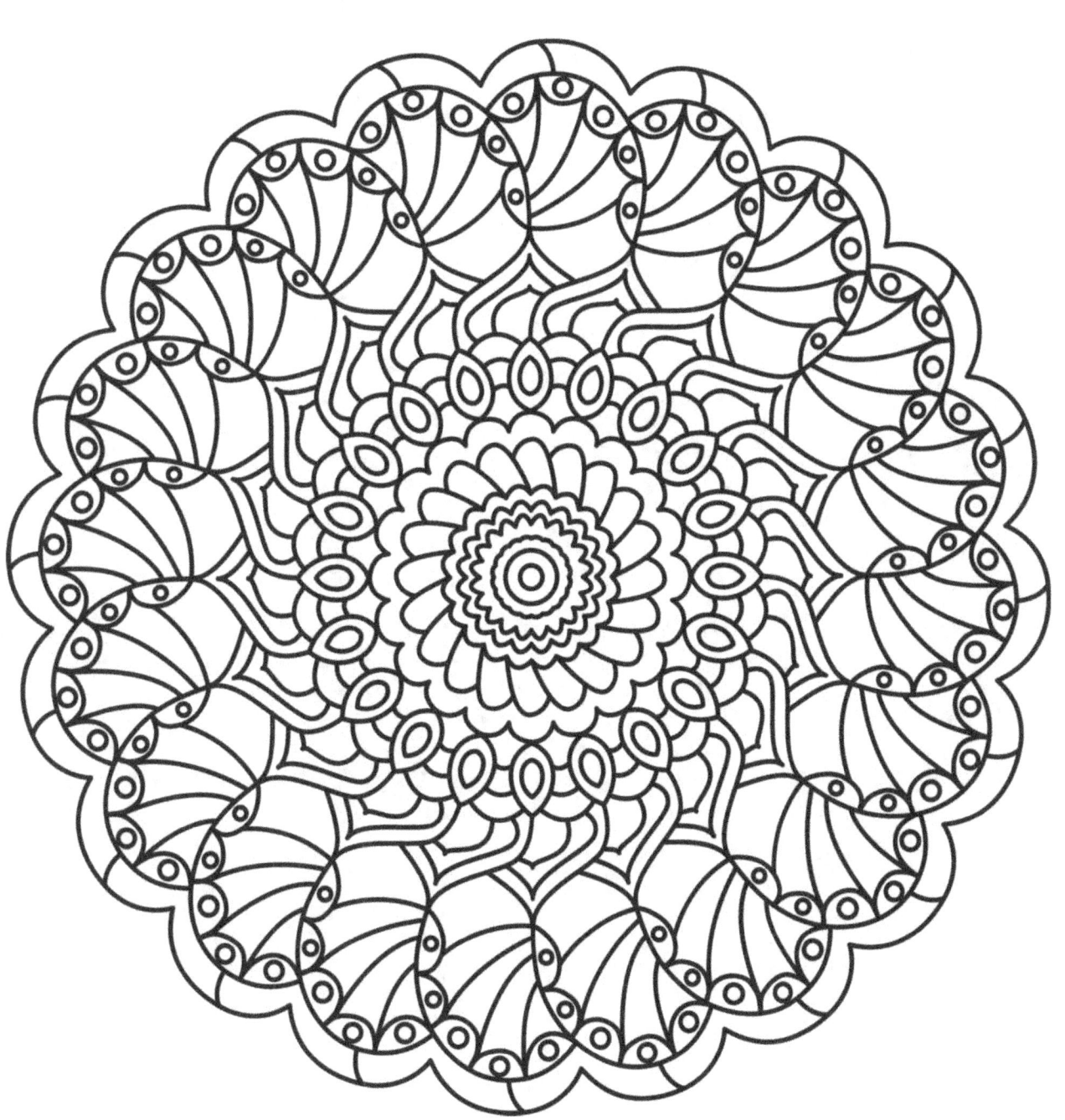

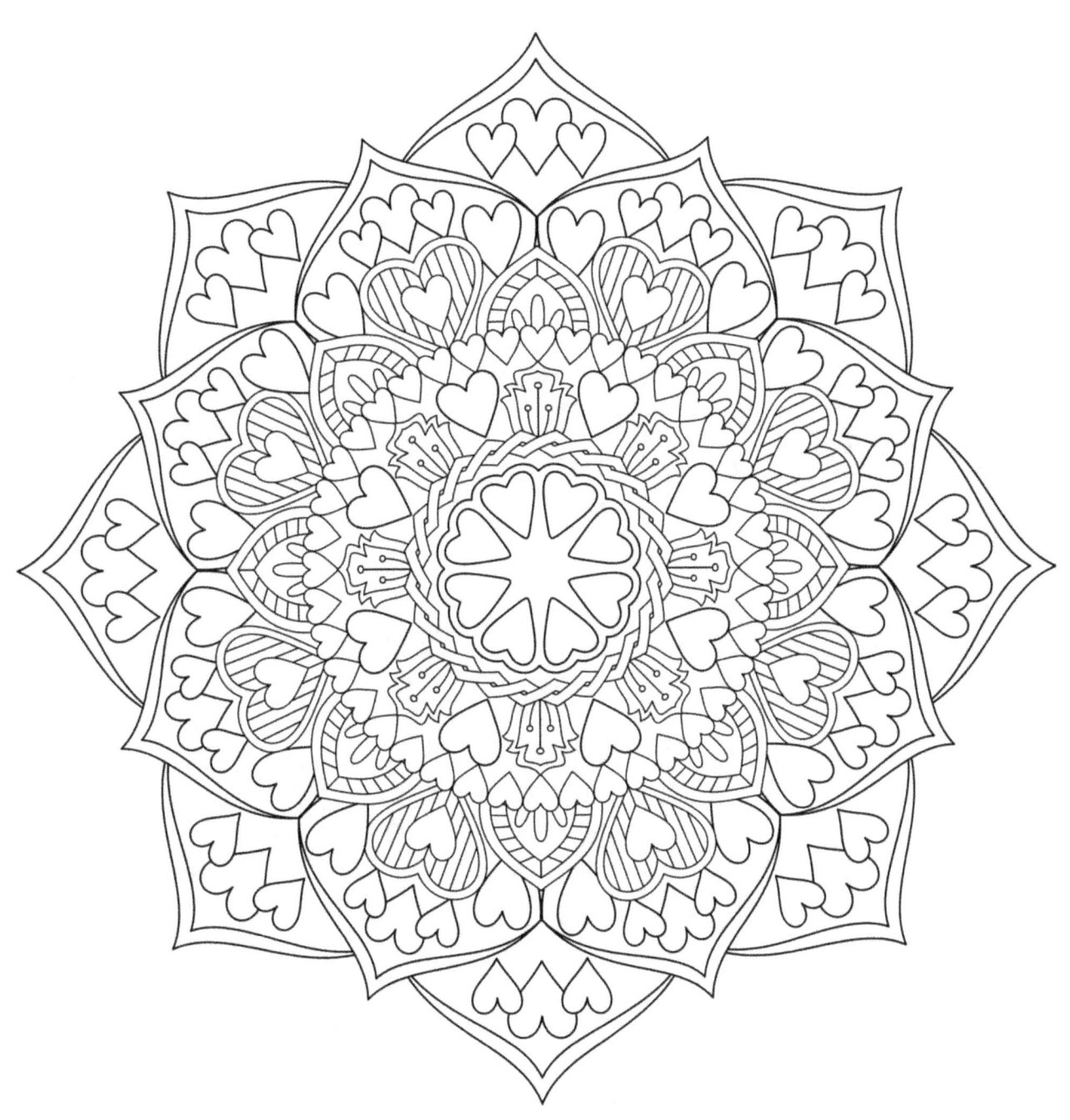

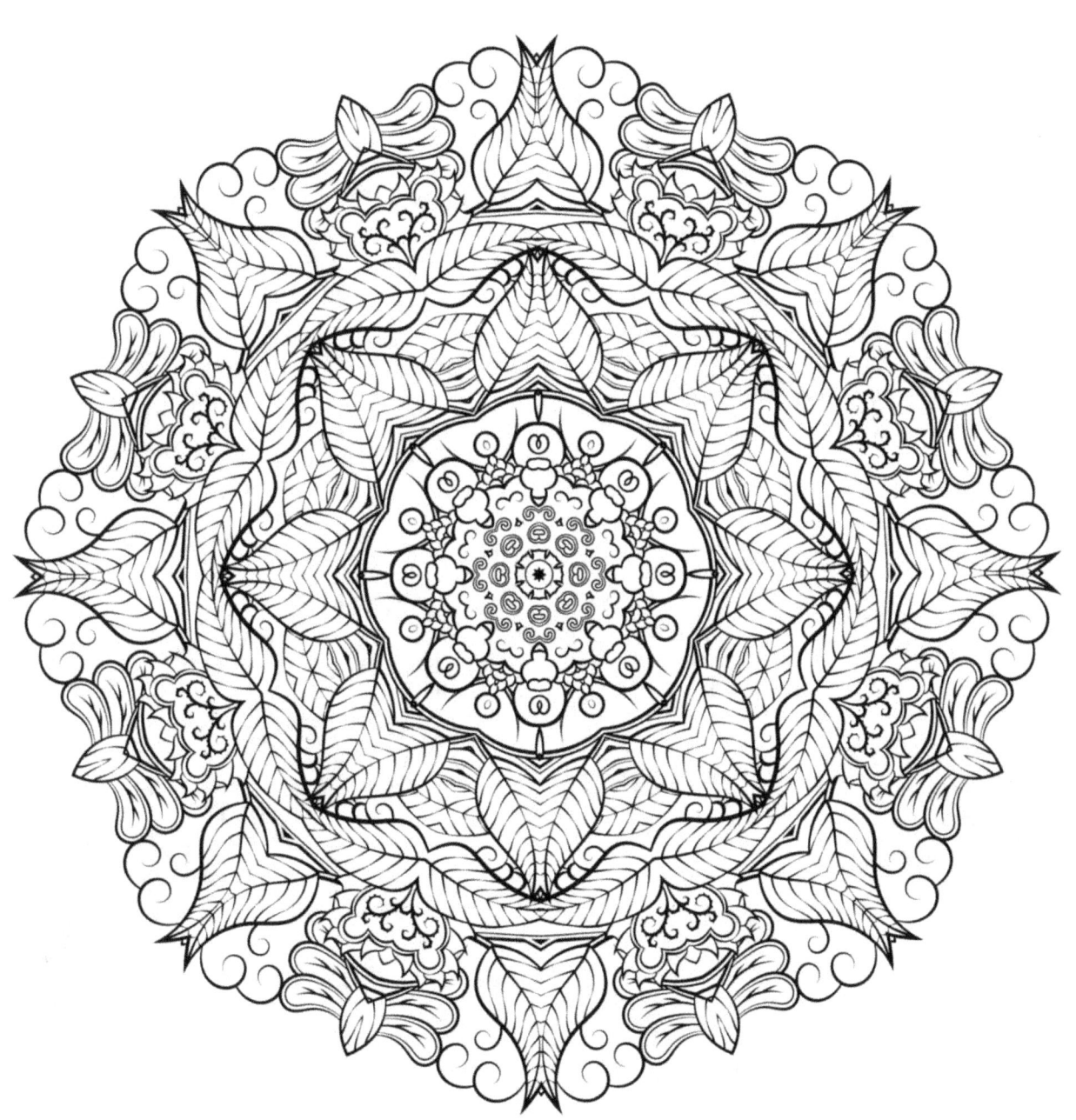

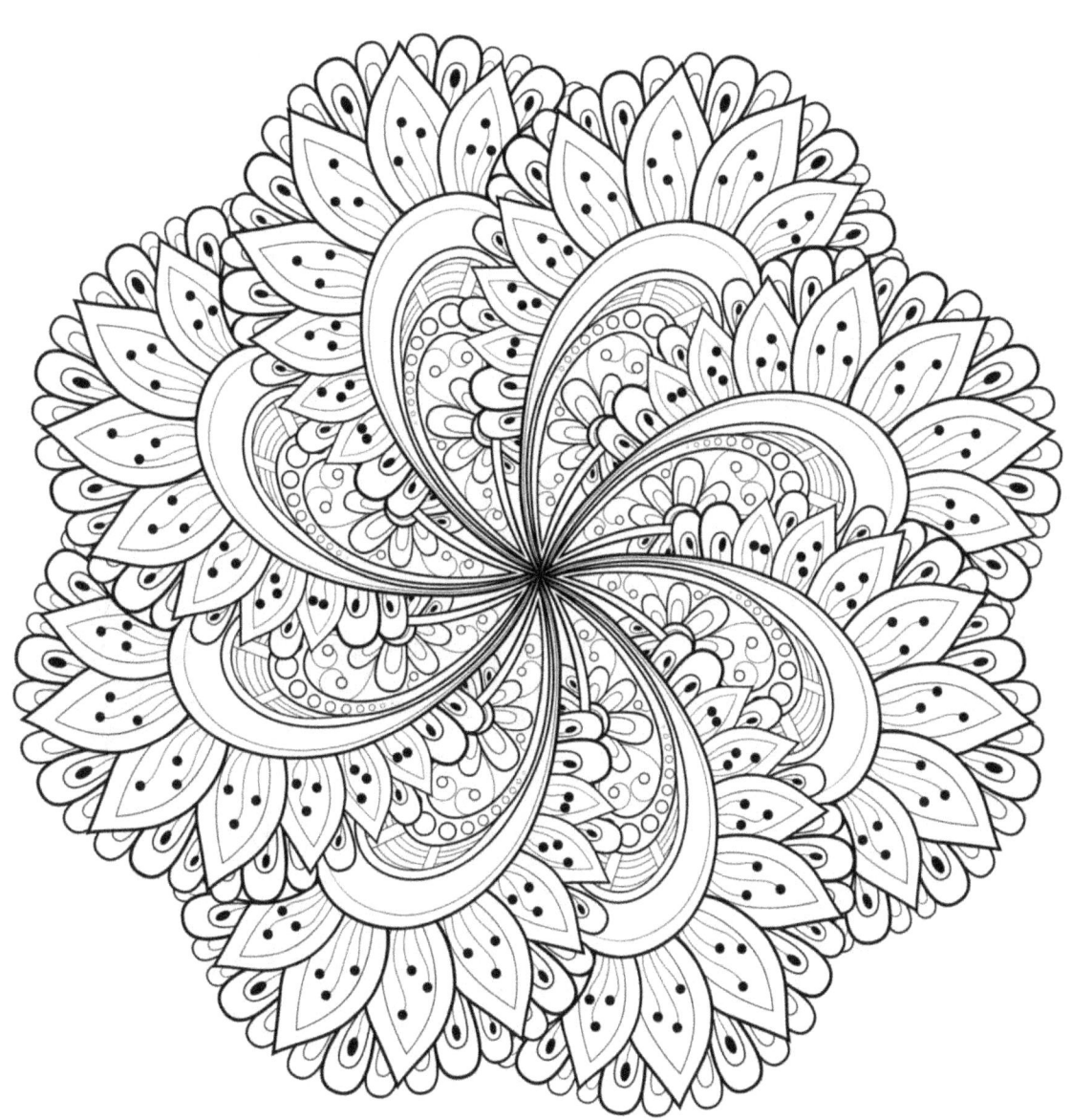

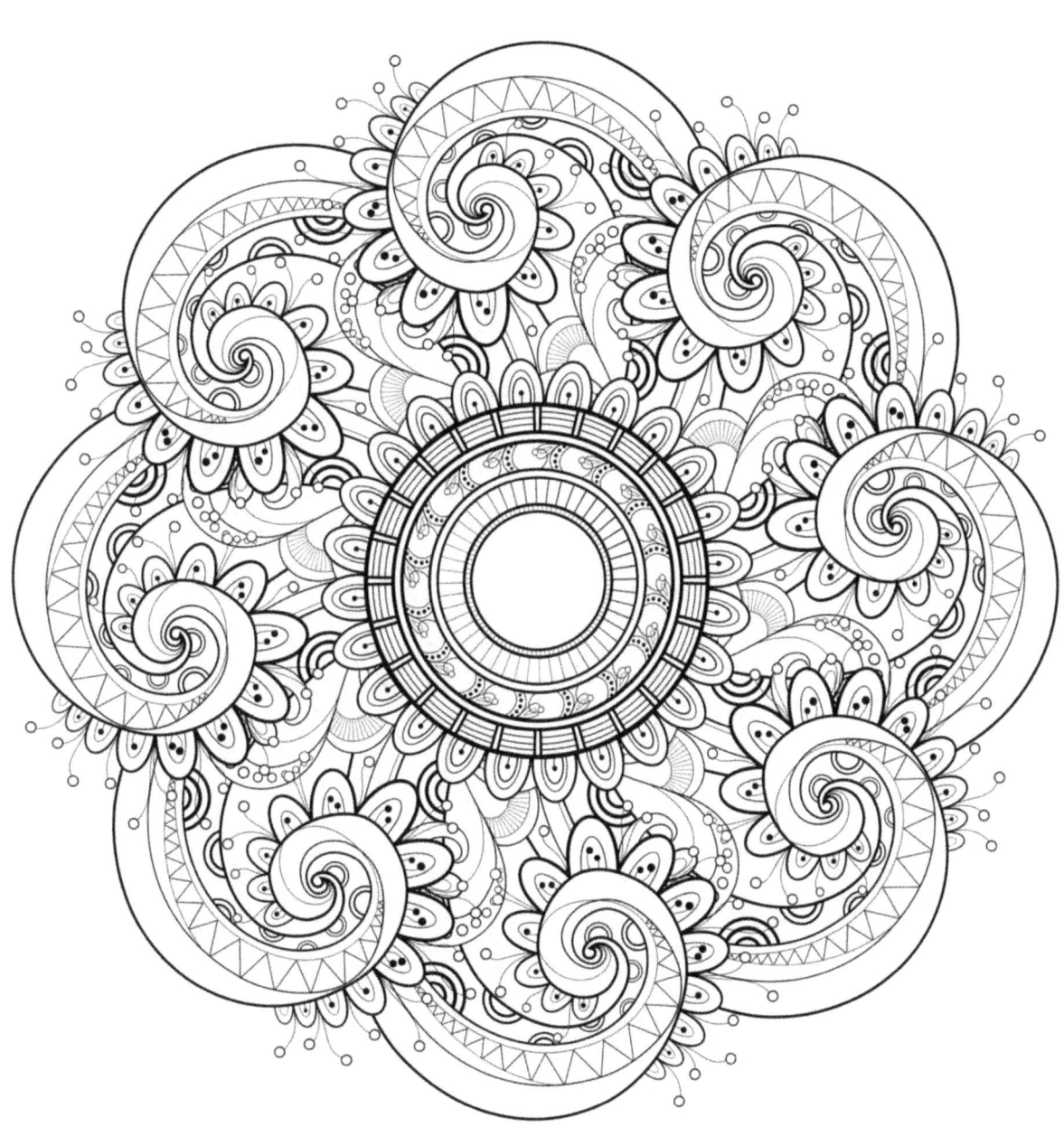

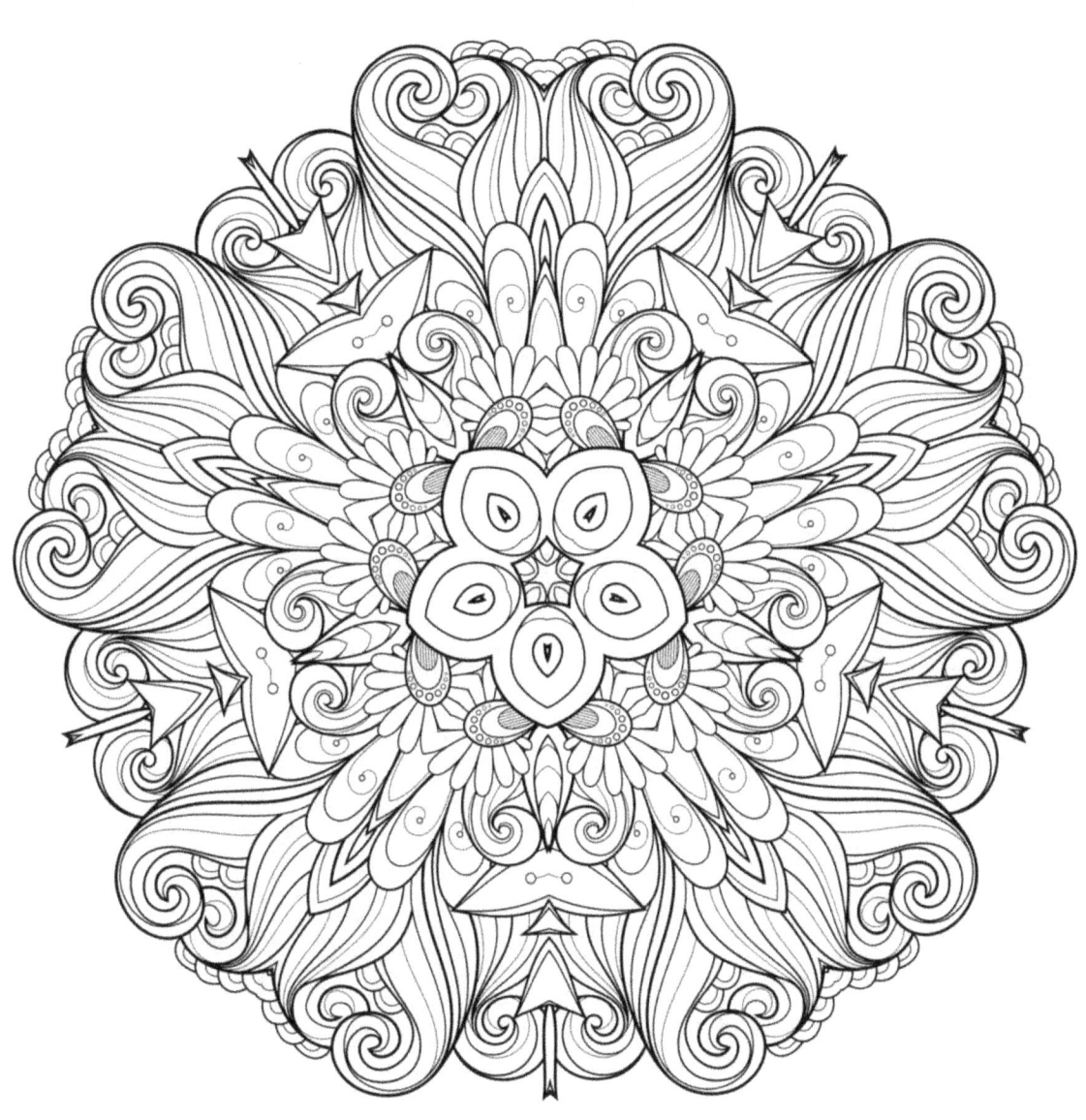

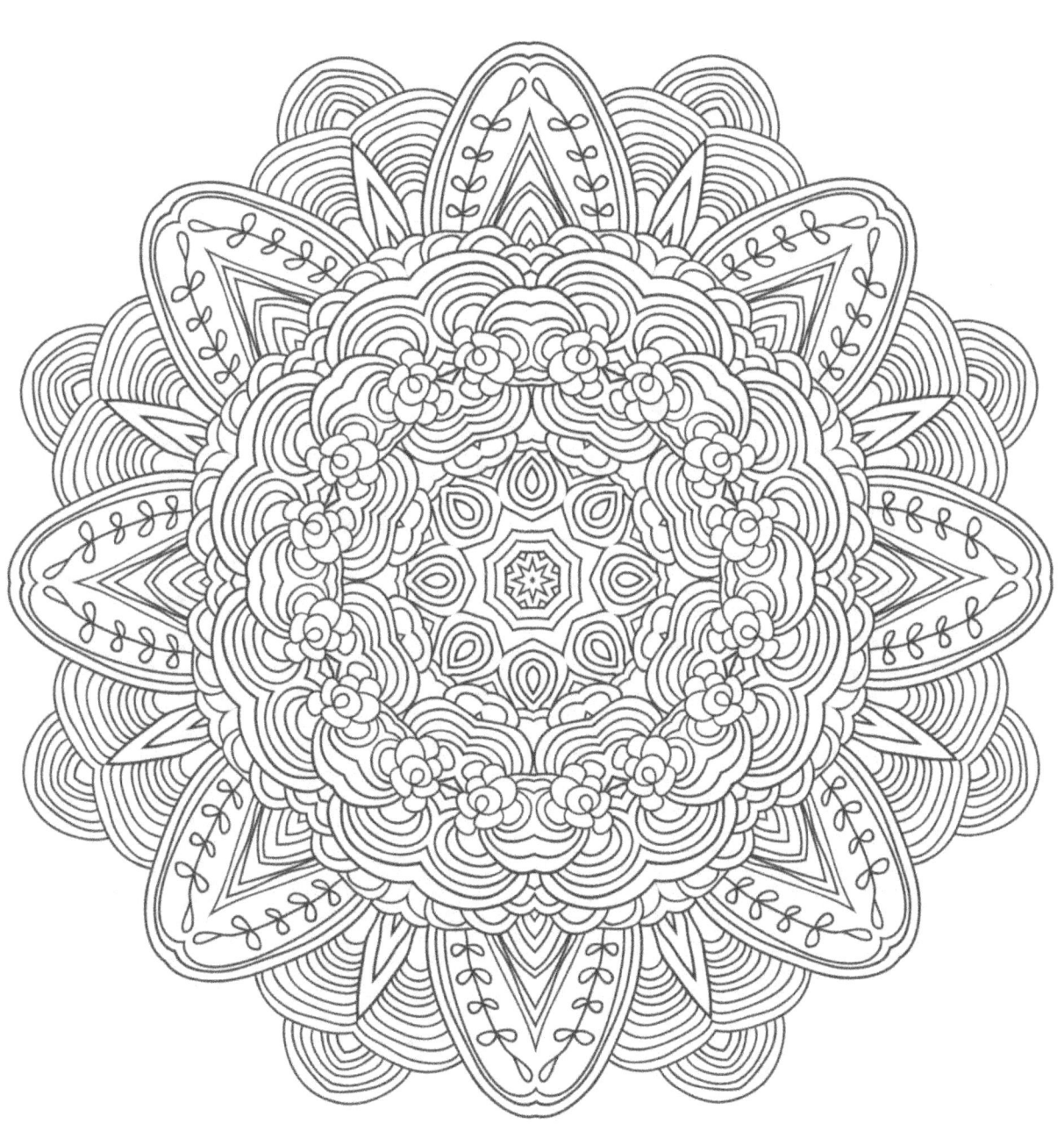

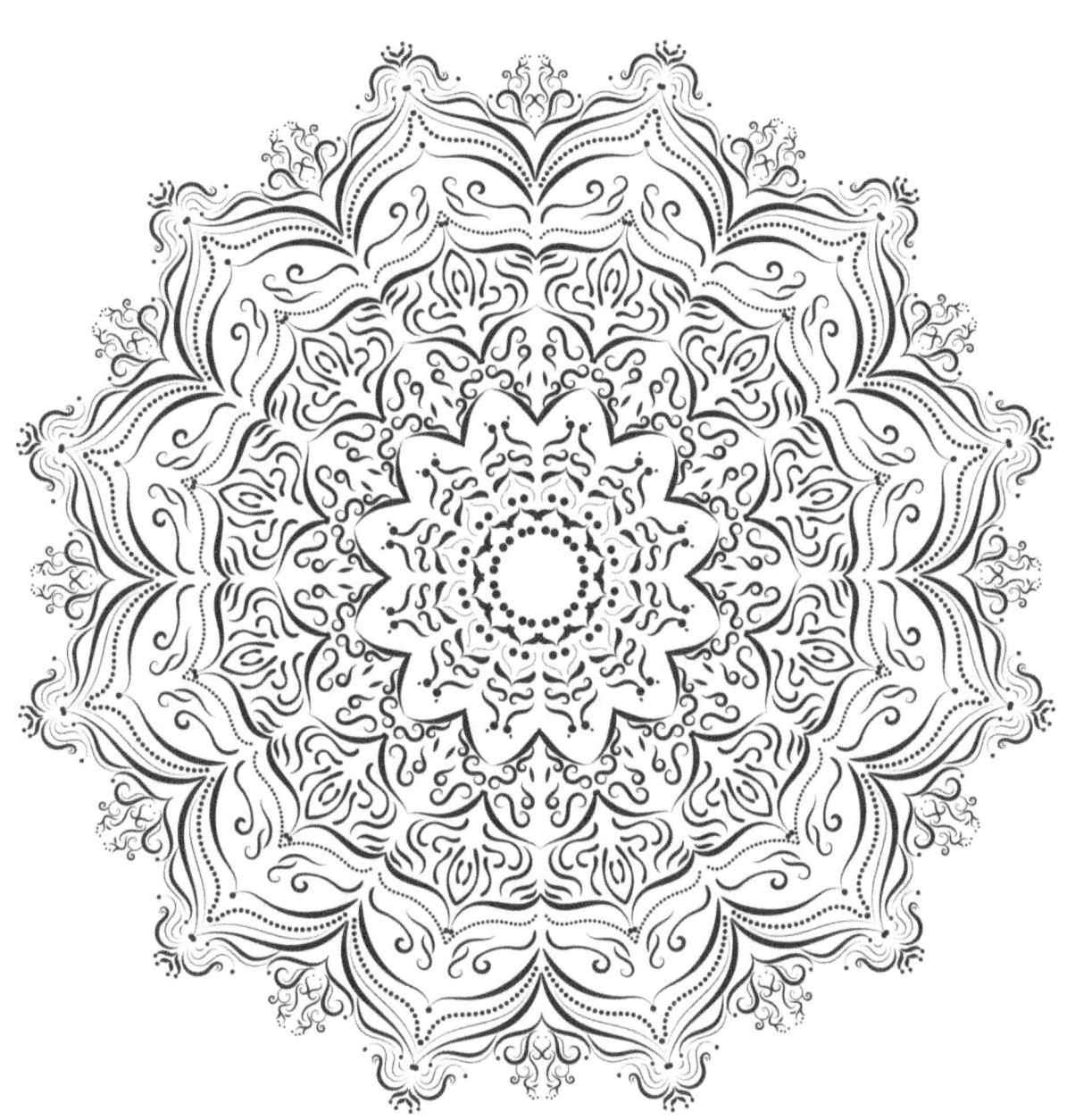

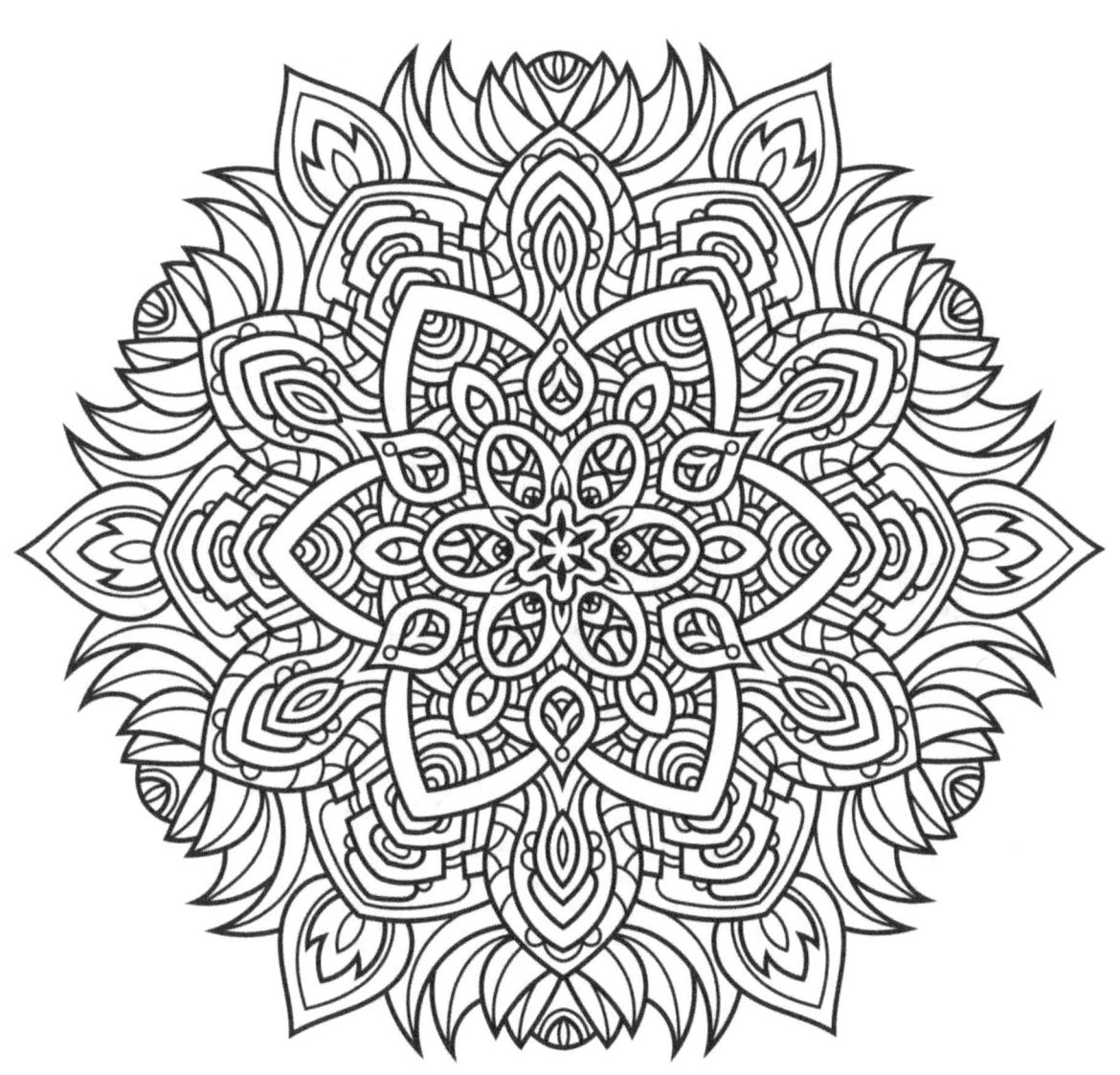

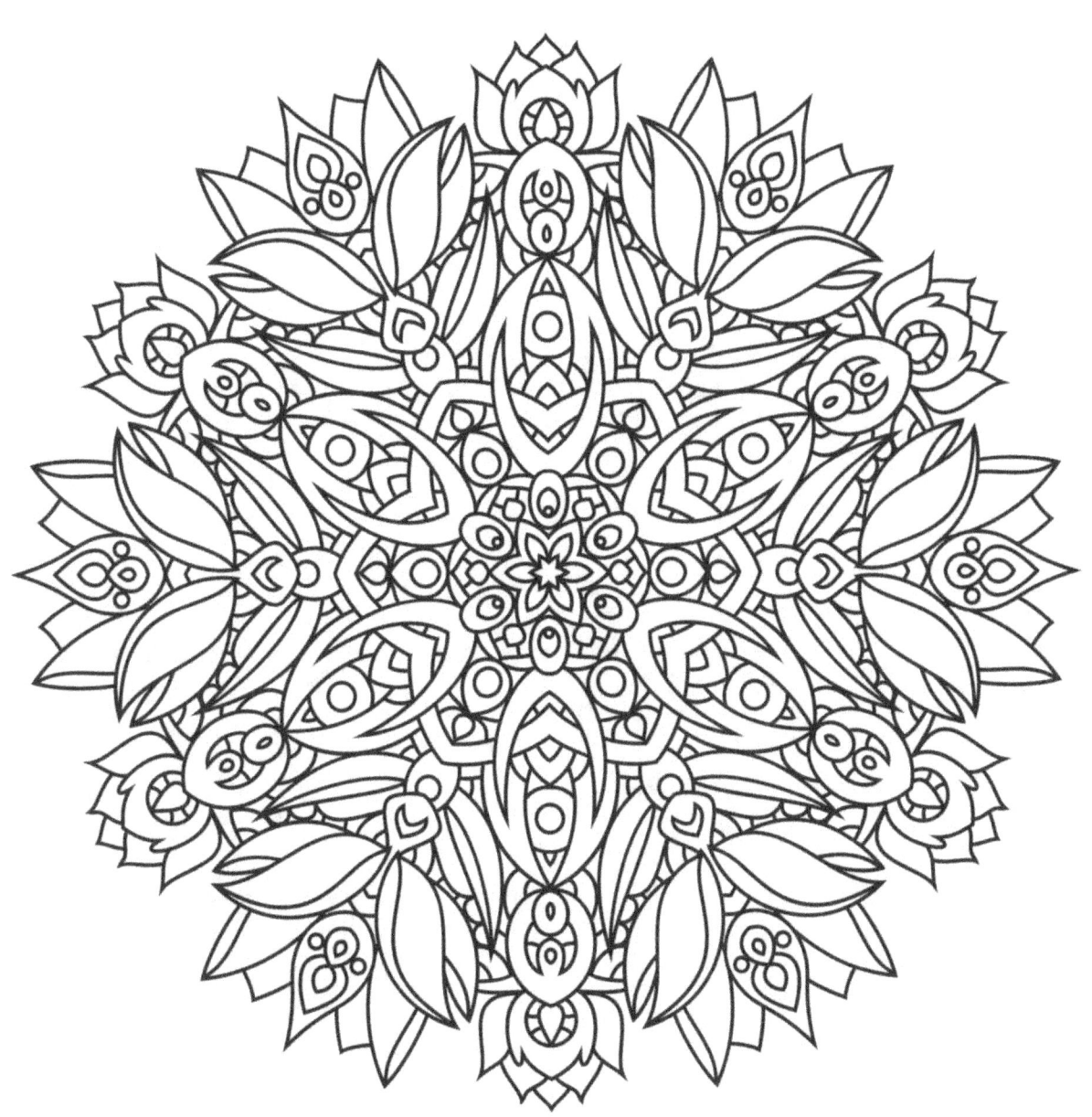

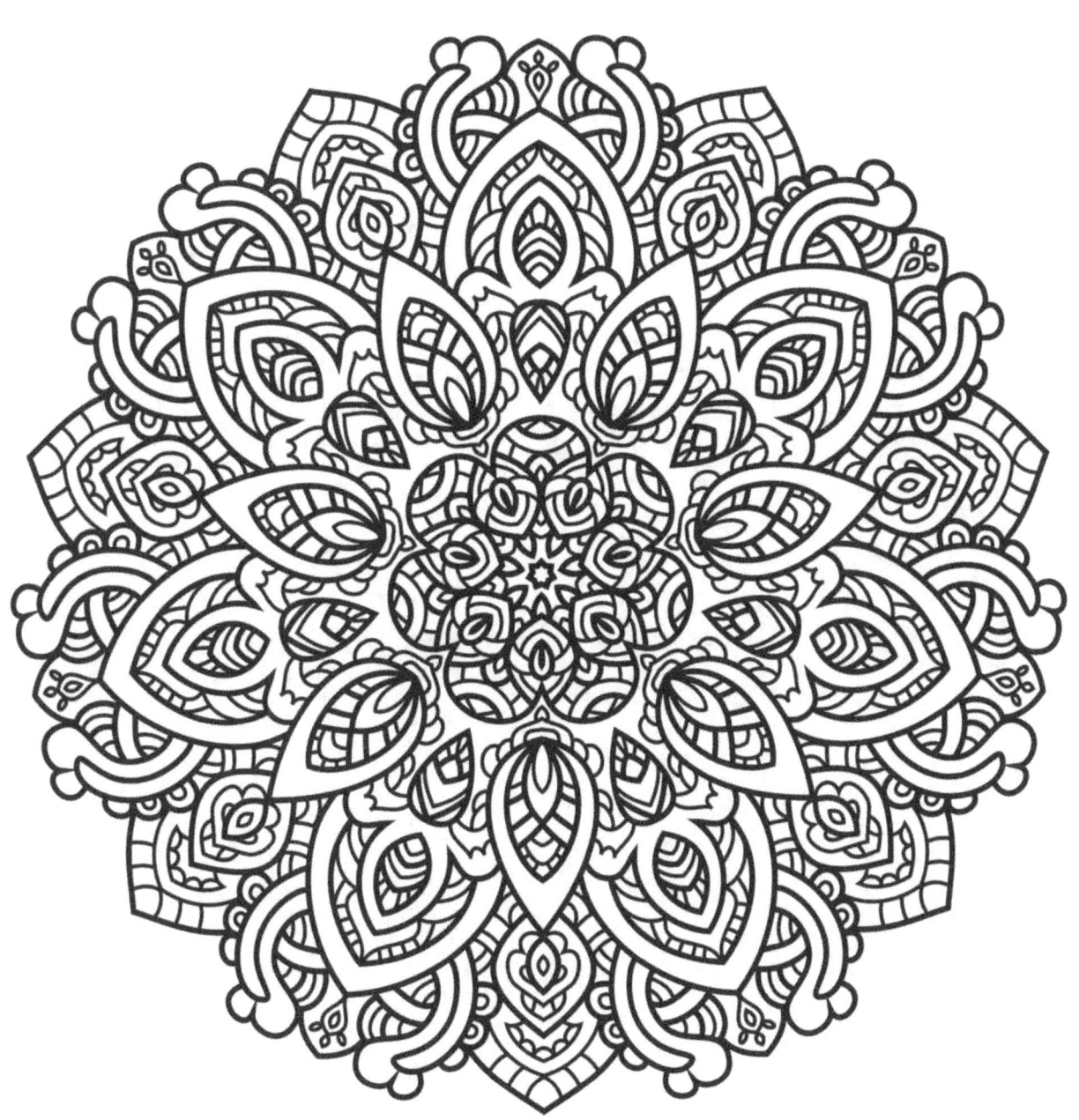

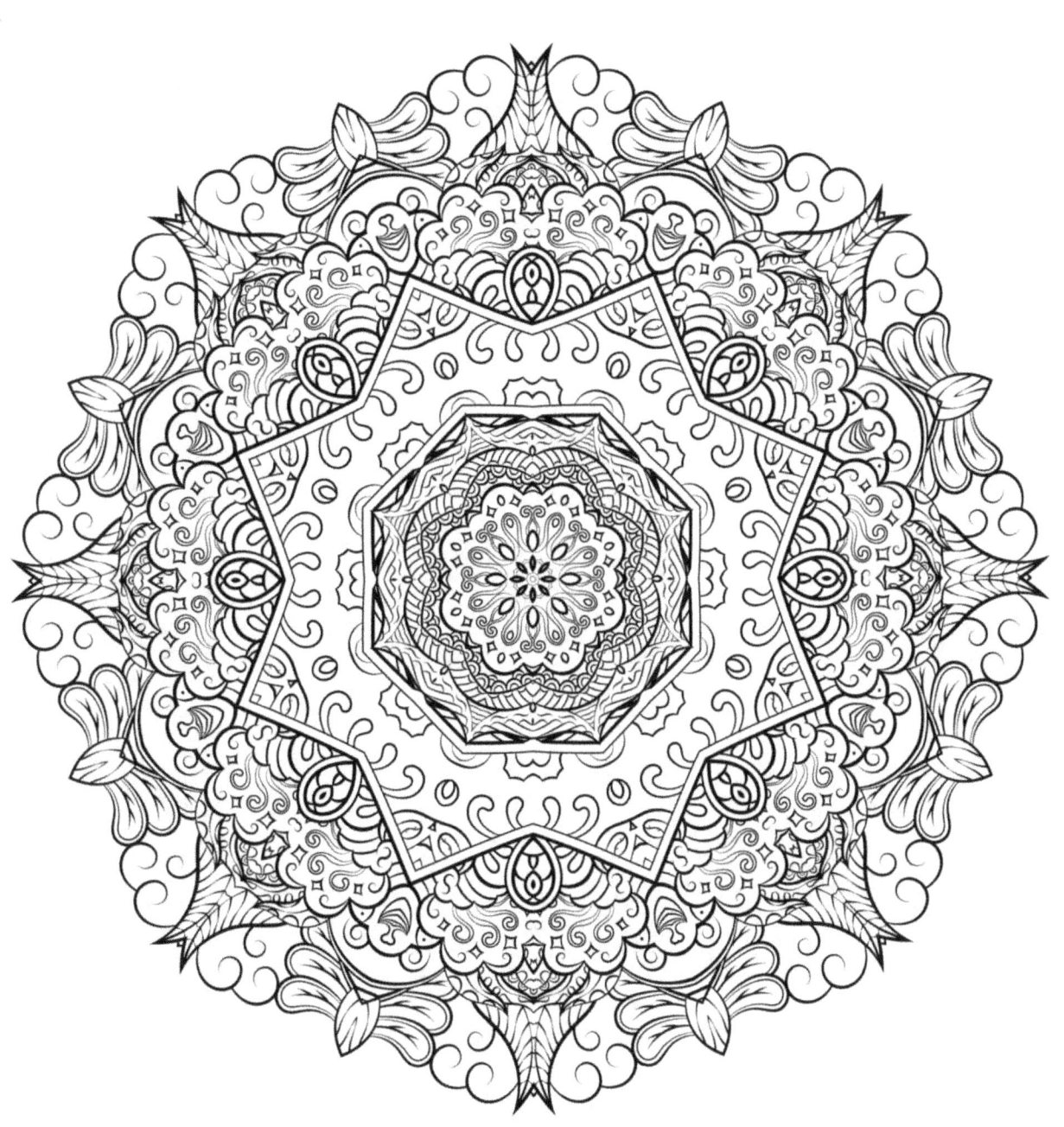

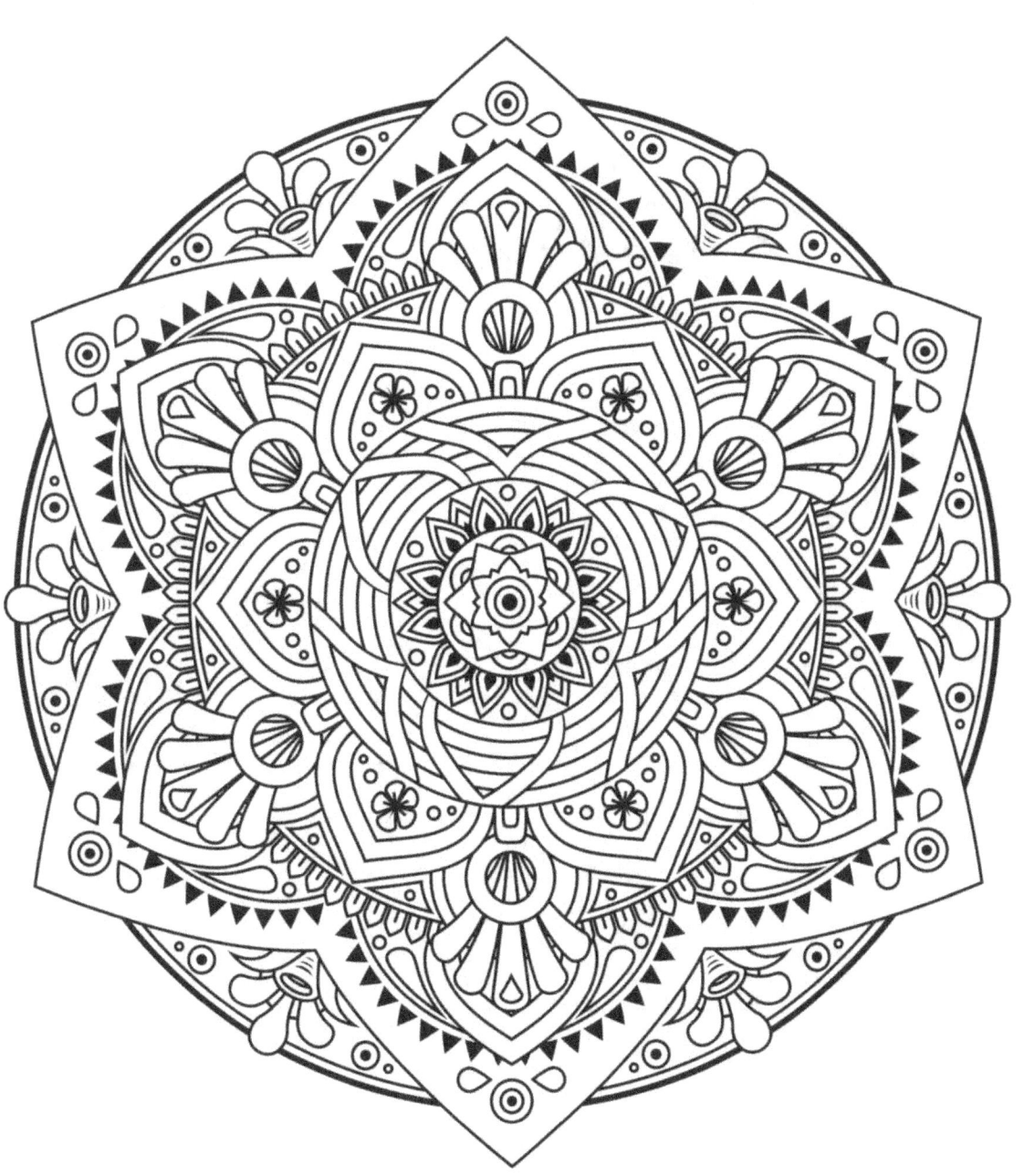

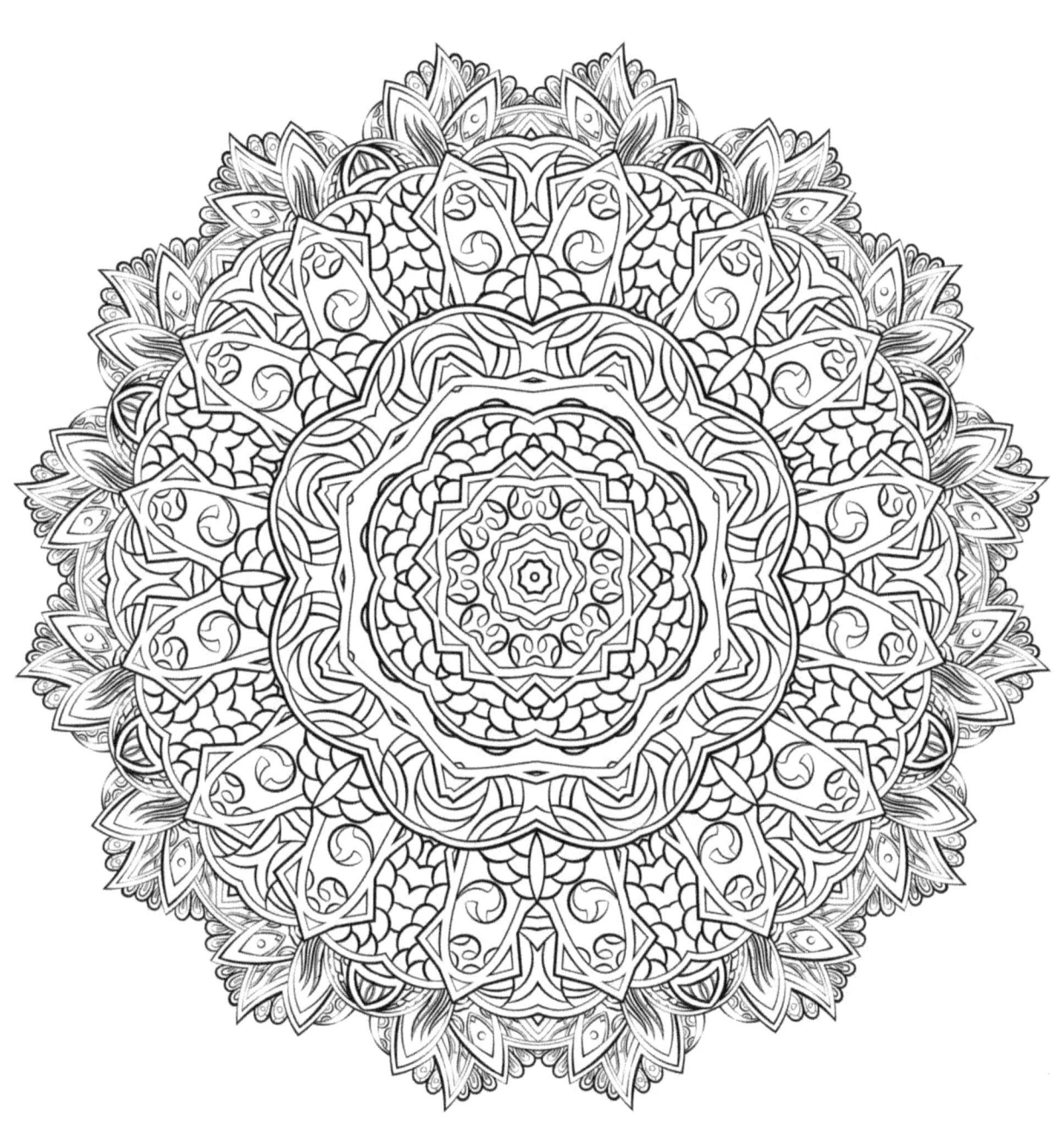

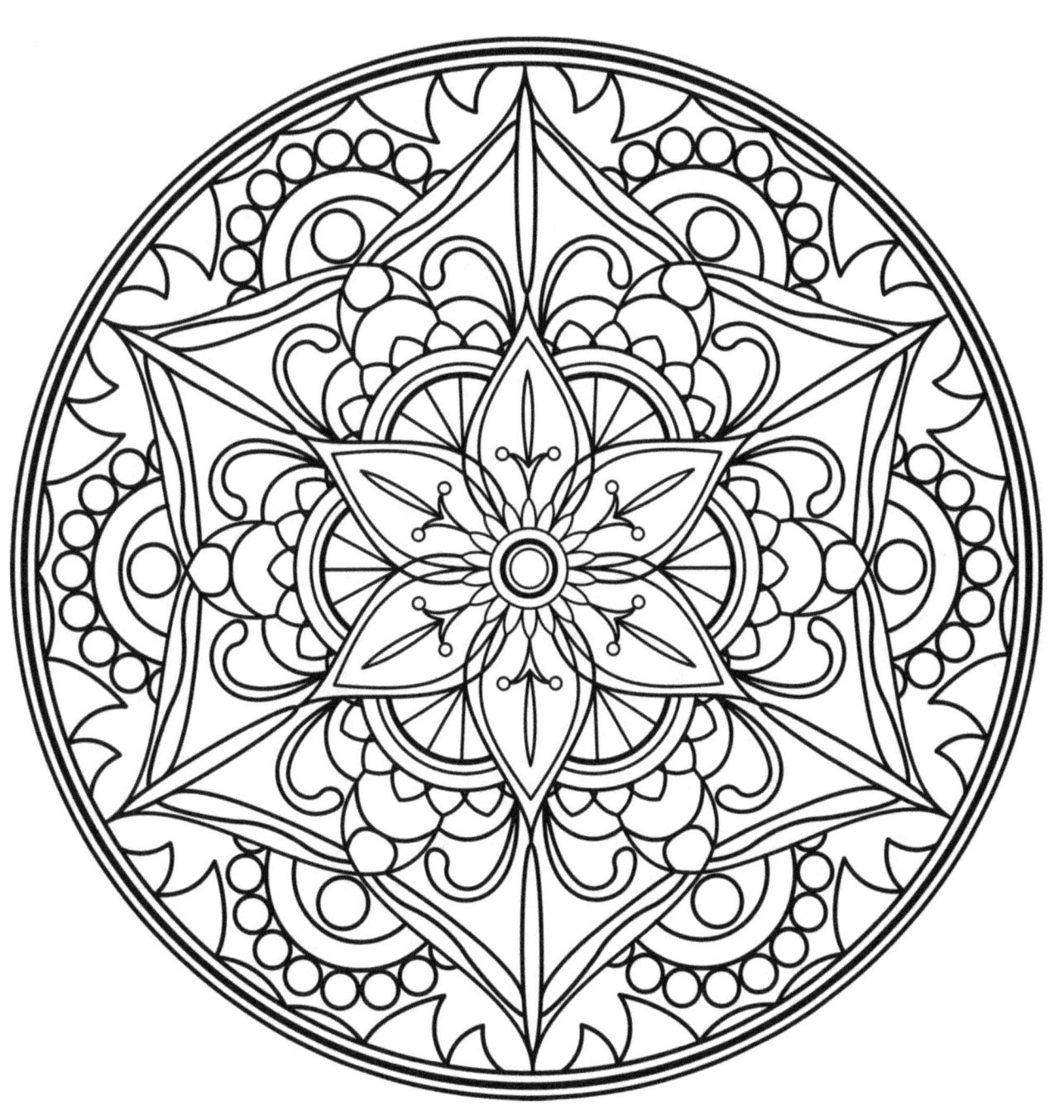

www.ingramcontent.com/pod-product-compliance
Lightning Source LLC
Chambersburg PA
CBHW080507220526
45465CB00006B/2405